LAW & THE ARTS-
ART & THE LAW

LAW & THE ARTS—
ART & THE LAW

Tem Horwitz   Assistant Editor, Timothy Patenode

Lawyers for the Creative Arts/Chicago

0594313 2

First Edition
First Printing

ISBN 0-914090-71-2
Library of Congress Catalog Card Number 79-54026

Book Design & Typography by Siemens Communication Graphics
Cover design by Joseph Essex

DEDICATION

Special thanks to the following for their support:

National Endowment for the Arts
Illinois Arts Council
Chicago Council on Fine Arts, the City of Chicago,
& Mayor Jane Byrne

This book is partially supported by grants from these agencies.

Contents

Introduction

This series of essays on LAW & THE ARTS comes out of almost a decade of experience working with artists and with arts groups. In a sense this book is a distillation of the experiences of the attorneys and staff of Lawyers for the Creative Arts/Chicago. It is an attempt to answer the questions that are asked most frequently, to suggest solutions to the most recurrent problems, and to highlight the common pitfalls into which the unwary artist may fall.

I have not attempted to impose a single style on the authors, believing that the approach, attitude, and the amount of detail in each chapter should be in harmony with the subject matter about which the individual authors are writing. Len Rubin, in his chapter on "Film & Video", gives an overview and suggest the complex web of issues with which filmmakers and video artists must deal. In a similar way, attorney/agent Jerry Wexler tries to educate the "new author" to the workings of the publishing industry and the role of the agent. On the other hand, Jane Shay Lynch, probes more deeply into the specific legal problems of the writer. Chapters on income tax, record keeping, bookkeeping, setting up and running not-for-profit corporations present both the overview and the detail.

It is not possible in a book with this breadth to exhaustively explore all of the areas of arts law, and to delve into the host of business, accounting, and legal problems of the artist. We have tried to cover all of the major issues, to highlight common problems, and to suggest those issues that should be explored by the artist or attorney in greater depth.

At Lawyers for the Creative Arts we are used to dealing with the barn door problem after the horses have escaped. This book is an attempt to remedy this situation bv encouraging the artist to handle his or her affairs in such a way that they create a minimum of problems for themselves, and to indicate when and why it is imperative to get legal counsel.

Special thanks to the NEA, the IAC, the CCFA, Ellen Mazer, Curt Matthews, Les and Barbara Siemens, Tim Patenode, and LCA's more than two hundred volunteer attorneys and accountants.

Tem Horwitz
Chicago, 1979

Writers & the Law

What Is a Copyright?

A copyright is a governmental grant, an acknowledgment that original writings are owned by the author. A copyright is the legal recognition of the special "property rights" in an author's work.

What Kinds of Writing Does a Copyright Protect?

Copyright protection is available for almost all writing —books, short stories, magazine articles, newspaper columns, poetry, plays, screenplays, and songs. Both fictional and nonfictional works are covered, and copyright protection is even available for such writings as an index, a master's thesis, a map, even an original directory, such as the phone book, or a name and address guide to vegetarian restaurants.

What is not protected? In the language of the copyright law, "words and short phrases" will not be. A catchy slogan, a clever word—if you are using these in business as a brand name for a product, or as the name of your musical group or other business, protection for the single word or short slogan may be available under the *trademark* laws, but not the copyright laws.

What else is not protected? Lists of ingredients are not, hence, the major part of most recipes. Does this mean that you have no protection if you write a cooking article or cookbook? No, because your article or book as a whole presumeably contains more text than a string of ingredients, affording you a basis for copyright protection.

The same principle applies to chemical formulae, and to math problems. Copyright law won't allow these to be removed from the "public domain", so an individual equation, such as $E = MC^2$, even if developed today under the new copyright act, would not be protected under the copyright laws. However, your math book or chemistry text would contain far more than a string of formulae or equations, and would, as a whole, be protected.

Computer programs—software—is an area where the copyright laws are up in the air. Right now, software is probably not protected under the copyright laws, but this situation may soon change. Oddly, the Copyright Office appears to be accepting software for copyright registration, the same as any written work. However, if your allegedly copyrighted software program is infringed, it is doubtful that the copyright will be of any use to you in an infringement suit. CONTU (The National Commission on New Technological Uses of Copyrighted Works), a congressionally organized advisory body, is presently in the process of trying to resolve the computer software issue.

Will a Copyright Protect My Idea?
No!

A copyright protects the specific way that you develop, detail and express your idea in writing. That is, if you have an idea for an article about nuclear-powered musical instruments of the future, you can't obtain protection for your *concept*. Anyone can use your idea, and can write, copyright and publish his or her own article about nuclear-powered musical instruments of the future.

However, if somebody else wants to write an article dealing with the same subject or idea of *your* copyrighted article, that second somebody had better not lift sentences or paragraphs from your article, and had better not even paraphrase your article, or parts of it, because that would be copyright infringement.

How Original Must My Writing Be
To Gain Copyright Protection?

Not very!

The Copyright Office does not make an extensive examination of the substance of your work, because what you are keeping from the public domain is your way of expressing a concept, which concept anyone is entitled to use in his or her own words. That is, your "monopoly" does not work a serious hardship on the public, so your work does not have to pass serious muster to earn its copyright protection. Obviously, if your work was primarily copied from a public domain work and you find yourself holding a certificate of copyright registration nonetheless, an "infringer" you seek to sue over the matter can raise a public domain defense, despite your registration.

How Different Does Something Have to
Be from a Copyrighted Work
in Order Not to Infringe?

Substantially different!

Rumors—all false—abound that "a ten per cent change" is sufficient, or that changing the main character from, say, Carl to Carla is sufficient or that relocating the action from San Francisco to Rio will protect against infringement. Such rumors are wrong, wrong, wrong.

The legal test of whether someone has copied your work is whether there is "substantial similarity" between the allegedly infringing work and your copyrighted one. Under the "substantial similarity" test, have people been found liable for copyright infringement if "all" they've done is paraphrase? Yes! Paraphrasing, under the copyright laws, is still plagiarism—infringement of copyright.

As we have discussed, an idea (or as the courts put it, a "mere naked idea") is not protectable. But what if there are already four thousand seventy-two articles on your chosen theme of, say, the conspiracy theory of the Kennedy assassination? Isn't your way of expressing yourself with respect to this idea going to collide with a previous copyrighted piece?

In some sense, yes, but you are entitled to write about the incident, using all of the facts you need to do so. Obviously, you are not required to change Jackie's name to Judy, or to move the murder site to Tacoma just to avoid duplication of these facts in a prior work. The law favors "independent creation." If it is clear that you have not copied or paraphrased the other articles, you'll not be penalized for redundancy!

Does "independent creation" mean that if you should *unconsciously* come too close to a copyrighted work, you're off the hook due to your good faith? No, especially if the copyright owner can prove that you've had access to the copyrighted work.

The case against George Harrison is a good example of an *innocent* infringer being found liable for copyright infringement. You may remember that Harrison's "My Sweet Lord" was charged to be an infringement of "He's So Fine", the song made popular by the Chiffons. The court concluded that it was likely that Harrison had *subconsciously* copied the work, despite all good intentions.

How about written fiction? If an idea can't be protected, can a plot? No, *if* you view a plot as merely the most pared-down skeleton, without detail or characterization or development, such as "boy meets girl, boy moves to big city, an urban/financial crisis occurs which causes boy to realize the small town life is the good life, boy goes back to girl, who (a) has married another, or (b) has made a new life for herself."

But if your plot goes like this: "Boy (Fred) is a marine biologist. Girl (Julia) is a veterinarian, specializing in rare fish. Boy & girl live in resort town under the shadow of a UFO, causing boy to move to Nashville etc," or if your plot goes into Fred's family history, and Julia's bout with scarlet fever, and contains flashback episodes of the two with their respective fish, studying while the UFO hovers above the aquarium, then there is a difference. The difference is development, progression, *specifics*. The more developed a plot, the more willing a court will be to recognize that more than a "mere naked idea" has been stolen.

What If My Work Depends Upon a Prior Work— Let's Say I Want to Write a Play Based on the "Doonesbury" Cartoon Strip, or HAMLET?

The right to adapt a work into another medium or form belongs to the copyright owner, as does the right to translate into another language. Naturally, the copyright owner is entitled to give or to sell you permission to make the adaptation. We're all aware that authors will often sell movie rights, for example. These adaptations are known as "derivative works."

Let us say you do get written permission from an author to write and produce your play based on his or her work. Can your particular adaptation be protected by copyright? Yes! Sometimes part of your agreement with the author of the "underlying work"—the first, or original version—is that you provide that that author is to own the copyright in your version. If your agreement does not so provide, then you own the copyright in your version.

Now, as to *Hamlet*, let us say you want to make a modern version, pointing out the day's ills, but using the basic characterization of the original. This you may do freely. Why? Shakespeare's work is in the public domain. Just make sure you've not copied from someone else's—current and copyrighted—modern version of *Hamlet*. And yes, your new version, insofar as it's original, is copyrightable, and you may protect it from infringement.

But What about "Fair Use"?

Fair use, as defined by Marybeth Peters, senior attorney/ advisor to the Copyright Office, "allows copying without permission from, or payment to, the copyright owner where the use is reasonable and not harmful to the rights of the copyright owner." However, what is "reasonable" and "not harmful" is not necessarily determined by your personal beliefs.

Fair use is one of the most nebulous, tricky areas of the Copyright Law, since the same conduct is viewed differently depending on *who* is taking the copyrighted material from *where*, and to *what end!*

For example, your use of chunks of material from a copyrighted work, properly credited to the copyright owner, might be "fair use" in your doctoral thesis. But your use of the exact same chunk of quoted material, even if credited to the copyright owner, could get you into hot water if it is included in your article for the *Chicago Tribune*.

Why? In determining "fair use" the courts look to the "purpose and character of the use, including whether such use is of commercial nature, or for educational purposes".

In the example above, the use on a Broadway stage of a line or two from "Doonesbury" would probably *not* be excused as "fair use." On the other hand, use of half a dozen of the lines in a high school play might well be excused as fair use. But, when you quote without permission, there are no guarantees, and the law of fair use operates on a continuum. That is, in our example, fifty lines, even in the high school class play, would likely exceed the bounds of fair use.

Because of the ill-defined, continuum nature of fair use, there is no rule advising how many words you may quote before crossing the border from fair to unfair use. Again, you could quote more in a thesis than in a *Cosmopolitan* magazine feature. But in addition to the type of piece you've prepared, and the number of words you've quoted, fair use depends upon the percentage of quoted material in relation to the work as a whole from which the quote was taken. That is, if you used half of a two hundred-word copyrighted article you're on shakier ground than if you'd used one hundred "borrowed" words from a 20,000 word book.

Another fact is timeliness. If you've had 6 months' lead time, you're expected to have had the opportunity to contact the copyright owner whose work you'd like to quote. If your article is due at the printers in two days, however, and you want to add a quoted sentence or two from someone's article published this morning, the courts may conclude that your failure to obtain permission for use of the small quote was reasonable.

Does attributing the quoted portion to the author relieve you of liability for copyright infringement? No, but the re-verse—*omitting* the author credit—may well make your copying appear to be intentional plagiarism, so that the equitable defense of fair use won't apply. Fair is fair. Also, as a practical matter, a quoted author is less likely to feel ripped off if properly credited, and, accordingly, is less likely to sue you.

We are discussing lawsuits because "fair use" does not automatically prevent an irate author or publisher from suing you and/or your publisher for copyright infringement with respect to the quoted material. Fair use merely permits you a defense—an excuse—to tell the judge if suit is filed.

How about Parody—How Can I Evoke the Original Without Infringing on It?

Naturally, your parody of someone else's copyrighted work is, in a sense, a fanciful parody of it. As even paraphrasing is forbidden by the copyright laws, how can you spoof on another's work? The courts have, over the years, recognized parody as a legitimate art form, and have carved out certain "gut reaction" exceptions to the infringement laws. The courts often cite that a parody is permitted to "recall and conjure up the original," but must add a contribution of its own.

When is this a problem? When there are aspects of unfair competition involved, or serious disparagement of another's copyrighted work.

That is, if the parody is such that the public might actually think the original author created it, the author may have a valid claim against the parodist. Sometimes, the very artistry of a parody is in its line-by-line adherence to the original. But this the courts have found unacceptable. An example from the comic book genre illustrates that point. Recently, after a court battle lasting some five years, and resulting in several court opinions, a group of cartoonists, The Air Pirates, were found liable for copyright infringement for their comic book showing Walt Disney characters enjoying sex and drugs. The

Court was impressed with the argument of The Air Pirates that the beauty of their parody was in the near-duplication of the Disney works parodied. Argued the parodists, a less precise rendition would have destroyed the humor. Nevertheless, the Court concluded that, despite no intention on the part of the authors to have anyone believe the comic book came from Disney Studios, the copying disparaged the work, and it came too close to the copyrighted drawings.

If your parody involves a *product* rather than a literary piece, you may run into "unfair competition" problems, as the makers of the new board game *ANTIMONOPOLY* learned when they were successfully sued for trademark infringement of, and unfair competition with, MONOPOLY.

Also related is the spoof which, while not copyright infringement, is viewed as sufficiently damaging to the "spoof-ee" to warrant judicial relief. An example is the recent decision enjoining further distribution of the skin flick, "Debbie Does Dallas," in which actresses in uniforms resembling those of the Dallas Cowgirl cheerleaders were portrayed in the style to which that film genre is accustomed. In that case, the judge defined parody and satire, and concluded that *this* film did not pass muster:

"A parody is a work in which the language or style of another work is closely imitated or mimicked for comic effect or ridicule. A satire is a work which holds up the vices or shortcoming of an individual or institution to ridicule or derision, usually with an intent to stimulate change; the use of wit, irony or sarcasm for the purpose of exposing and discrediting vice or folly.

"In the present case, there is no content, by way of story line or otherwise, which could conceivably place the movie "Debbie Does Dallas" within any definition of parody or satire. The purpose of the movie has nothing to do with humor; it has nothing to do with a commentary, either by ridicule or otherwise, upon the Dallas Cowboys Cheerleaders. There is basically nothing to the movie "Debbie Does Dallas" except a series of depictions of sex acts. The other phases of the movie—the dialogue and the "narrative"—are simply momentary and artificial settings for the depiction of the sex acts." *Dallas Cowboys Cheerleaders, Inc. v. Pussycat Cinema, Ltd.,* 201 U.S.P.Q. 740, 749 (S.D.N.Y. 1979).

The context in which your parody appears is also important. A short piece in a magazine spoofing a popular book would likely be more acceptable and less likely to be viewed as an infringement than would a *book* spoofing the book you've chosen as your subject of parody.

What about Personal Letters? My friend has become a candidate for President, and I want to publish a book of letters he wrote to me in 1968 when he was on acid.
The copyright in personal correspondence belongs to the person who wrote the letter, even without a copyright notice, and even if there was no indication that your correspondent meant to "reserve all rights" in them!

This principle was used with great success by an individual who won a copyright infringement suit against the government for stealing his mail, and "publishing" it—circulating it to the CIA and others.

Are There Special Fair Use Guidelines for Teachers and Librarians Who Frequently Photocopy Copyrighted Works?
Yes!

CONTU, with the assistance of educators and librarians, has developed certain guidelines which the courts respect, as to what constitutes "fair use" for teachers and librarians.

If you are a teacher or librarian—or an author concerned with what legitimate "fair use" copying may be made by schools and libraries of your work—write or telephone the copyright office, requesting brochures with respect to these teacher/librarian fair use guidelines.

Briefly, "fair use" cannot be a substitute for the purchase of available works, except in the case of single articles or cartoons or in a genuine emergency, and it is not an emergency if a school or library simply cannot afford to buy the work it is photocopying. If a teacher finds a timely article, he or she can photocopy one copy for each student in the class per term, but cannot re-use the article next term (because by then there will have been enough time to get permission of the copyright owner). Also, the school or school department cannot select the copyrighted piece to be shared under the "fair use" doctrine—an individual teacher must make this decision. Once the school administration or a department head gets involved, fair use ceases to be fair.

Well, what if my play is not based on "Doonesbury", but features a few backdrops using the "Doonesbury" strips, or has a few of the characters sitting around and reading from the copyrighted comic strip?
Get permission!

You are speaking here of a type of *collective work,* one which incorporates the work of others.

Generally, the same rules apply as for the "derivative" work, or adaptation. That is, if the work you incorporate in your own story, article or play is the copyrighted work of another, permission is necessary. If your characters are reading from Shakespeare, or the Bible, then you do not need permission to include these works. As with the derivative work, your new work is protectable under the copyright laws. If your collective work includes material in the public domain, the public domain sections will still be in the public domain, but the "new matter" of your work will be fully protected.

How Do I Protect an Anthology?
An anthology is a common type of composite work. If you are preparing, say, an anthology of essays about pizza, you will need to obtain the prior permission of each copyright proprietor or owner of the articles you want to use.

Your collection of essays will then be the subject of a fresh copyright in your own name. This copyright protection prohibits others from using all the same pizza articles in a subsequent anthology, even if the second anthology author also has permission from each of the essayists.

Your right to protect an anthology is not absolute when

your selections are the tried-and-true obvious ones for an anthology in your genre. If you are preparing an anthology of modern American fiction, for example, you will be permitted to use many of the same stories, and in generally the same order, as other anthologies dealing with the same topic, even though the other anthologies are copyrighted as a unit. How to protect your own collection? The best way is to have careful text "linking" the succession of pieces. By creating a distinguishable new work, you'll enhance your scope of copyright protection.

How Do I Get a Copyright?
If you write it, you've got it.

Under the new copyright law you obtain copyright protection under the federal laws the instant you have completed your work. Without more. Without a copyright notice. Without publishing the work. Without registering the work in Washington.

The minute you put down your pencil, you pick up your copyright automatically, and whether you know it or not!

Then What Is a Copyright Notice for?
Under the old copyright law, if a work was published without proper notice, it went into the public domain. That is, with very rare exceptions, the old law took away copyright protection if a work was disseminated without a copyright notice, even by accident, or even if the work had the copyright notice on the wrong page. Under the old law, you could even write "this article is copyrighted to the author" on your piece, and could lose all your rights anyway, because such a statement is not a proper copyright notice.

While the copyright notice no longer has this life-giving and life-preserving significance, the new law still requires that your copyright notice appear on your published works. However, if you slip up, your work is *not* thrust into the public domain as a result. Rather, you have five years to put out a reprint bearing the correct notice. Also, the new law doesn't specify, as did the old one, a proper location for the notice. Any area where the notice can be seen, to give the public notice, is sufficient under the new law. The first page of your article, the title page of your book, would be reasonable.

Under the new law, if you see a relatively recent work without a copyright notice, how can you tell if it's in the public domain. You can't—or, more accurately, it isn't. Under the new law, lack of a copyright notice tells you *nothing* about the copyright status of a work created after Jan. 1, 1978. The copyright notice is desirable as a "no trespassing" sign to would-be infringers, warning that you know your rights.

Now, what is a proper copyright notice? The following is:

© Jane Shay Lynch 1979

This notice is sufficient to ensure protection in most countries. If you want protection in Latin America as well, add the following to your notice: "All Rights Reserved." The word "copyright" can, at your option, be added to the notice as an "extra strength" warning:

Copyright © Your name, 19____*

If the work is a collective work and contains earlier material, or is adapted from an earlier work, it is sufficient to include the year date you completed this collective or derivative work. However, in a collective work such as an anthology, each separately copyrighted article or story should ideally include its own copyright notice on the first page of each such article or story, and again on the inside front cover or credits section of the collective work.

For the Purposes of Copyright Protection,
What Is Your Name?
Seriously, under the old law, protection was lost because the copyright notice was in the name of a made-up entity that the author thought was amusing, or the copyright notice had

____

* Year date in which you completed the work

only the initials, not the name, of the owner. The new law is less harsh, because the "wrong" name can be corrected on subsequent editions. Still, if you are not well known by your initials, use your last name, or the pseudonym by which you are well known in the copyright notice.

What Is Copyright Registration and Why Is It Important?

Copyright registration is the government's acknowledgment of your claim to copyright. A record is made of the fact of your copyright, a number is assigned, and a certificate bearing that number is issued to you. The registration does *not* confer copyright status upon your work. Your mere creation of the work did that automatically under the new copyright law.

There is some public confusion as to the nature of copyright registration. People sometimes say they've "taken out" a copyright. Actually, they've *registered* their already existing copyrights, whether or not they realize it.

Registration is *not* required for your copyright to be valid. However, registration triggers some very important protections and is, therefore, desirable.

First, copyright registration is a prerequisite to bringing a lawsuit against the infringer of your copyrighted work. But it *is* permissible to obtain the copyright registration the day before you file suit, even though you knew of the infringement a year before you applied for registration!

Second, early registration can mean a big difference in the amount of damages (money) you'll be awarded if you win an infringement suit. If the copyright in your work was registered *before* the infringement began, you'll be entitled to opt for "statutory damages," an amount often larger than the "actual damages" you'd be restricted to if your copyright was not registered at the time of the infringement. Also, you're far more likely to be awarded the dollar amount of your attorneys fees and costs, in addition to your damage award, if your work was registered when the infringement took place.

Third—and this is especially important with respect to *unpublished* manuscripts—your certificate of copyright registration is "prima facie" evidence of copyright ownership and validity. That is, your certificate is the best evidence possible if there is any question concerning the date you created your work. This can be crucial if you want to establish that a publisher ripped off your unpublished manuscript.

Fourth, in the event that some other author wants to learn how to contact you, to get permission to quote your work in, say, a book, your registration provides your mailing address and the copyright office will provide a copy of your certificate to such persons.

As a footnote, I would mention that the new copyright act is one of the few laws that has been written "bisexually", so that the author is referred to as "his or her" throughout the entire statute.

How Do I Register My Copyright in a Book, Game, Story, Article, Play or Other Written Work?

First, obtain copyright form TX (or GPX, if you are an individual—not a corporation—seeking annual registration of all your published works for the previous year, as discussed below) from the Copyright Office, by writing:

United States Copyright Office
Library of Congress
Washington, D.C. 20559

The forms include detailed line-by-line instructions.

In addition, the Copyright Office will at your request send you brochures concerning copyright registration of the type of writing you're interested in.

You will note that the copyright form has a lengthy section headed TX/CON. Unless you are registering a long composite or collective work with many authors and references to other works, or the like, you will not need to fill in the TX/CON page.

I write so many things that if I had to spend the $10 registration fee on each unpublished work, I'd go broke. Any break in the Law?
Yes!

If your works are arguably related in theme, you can register a number of them as a "collective work," like an anthology. Poetry, short stories, short opinion pieces and the like lend themselves to this type of registration.

How about My Published Works, Can I Group Them Too?
Yes!

The new law gives a break to noncorporate freelancers who are published so regularly that the $10 fee would represent a hardship. If you have even a few pieces a year published, you are entitled to obtain a "group registration" at the end of twelve months, which will cover all of your published works for that period. The form to request from the copyright office is "GX" and they'll send you instructions for its use, as well.

What Is a "Common Law Copyright"?
Extinct!

Under the old law, a literary work could not be protected by the federal Copyright Act until it had been "published with proper notice." Accordingly, if your manuscript was ripped off you had to prove that you had never authorized "publication without notice." If you had made your manuscript widely available, and it bore no proper copyright notice, this was occasionally an adequate defense to an infringer under the old system.

The phrase "common law" simply means that there is no state or federal piece of *legislation*—statute—regulating the situation. (e.g. "common law" spouse) Now, the federal Copyright Act has abolished "common law" with respect to copyrights, and has *included* unpublished works in the federal statute.

What does this mean to you? For one thing, it means you are entitled to register your copyright in an unpublished manuscript, poem, or whatever.

The advantage of registering an *unpublished* work is that it is "prima facie" evidence of your creation of the work on the day indicated on the registration. That is, if you send in your manuscript to a motion picture company that, without your consent, uses your script in its next movie, how are you going to be able to prove that *your* creation came *first*? By registering your copyright before, or around the same time, that you send your manuscript around. That way, the Library of Congress has the evidence—and so do you.

Before it was possible to register an unpublished manuscript, writers sometimes sent themselves copies of their work by registered mail, to secure a postmark date as "evidence." Contrary to popular belief, there is *no* law specifying that this is satisfactory evidence. Far better is to take advantage of the new law, and have the federal evidence of earlier creation that the new law gives you.

To register a manuscript in an unpublished work, use form TX, as you would for a published work, and read the directions applicable to an "unpublished work," (called "Space 3: Creation and Publication.")

How Can I Protect Myself If I Send My Idea to a Magazine, Book Publisher or Motion Picture Company?
Remember, *ideas* per se are not protectable. And remember, to be more than an idea, a plot has to be fleshed out, with much detail and character development and so on.

Your best protection is not to send a page or two "idea." Rather, prepare a tightly developed long scene or section.

It is a fact of life that almost no book publisher, or television or motion picture studio, will purchase "over the transom" unsolicited manuscripts, unless you have an agent.

They don't have to—they get enough manuscripts from agents with whom they've dealt and who have proven themselves to be sources of potentially useable material.

Magazine publishers generally *will* look at, and purchase unsolicited works.

In any event, your best protection is to have a piece that is developed enough so that you are not merely sending off an "idea."

Back up your protection by protecting your un-published manuscript with a federal registration, which is prima facie evidence of your ownership, a copy of your manuscript being safely date-stamped and lodged with the Library of Congress.

Send your script or article registered mail, return receipt requested, so that there can be no question that the publisher or studio had access to your manuscript. Send a cover letter with your work, explaining that you are sub-mitting the work for possible purchase.

And do use your copyright notice (and the registration number of your unpublished work, if you have a registration) on the first page of the work.

When I Sell a Freelance Article to a Magazine, Do I Give Up All Further Rights to My Article?
No.

You sell only one-time use with respect to your un-solicited freelance work which is purchased by a magazine or newspaper publisher.

How about a Commissioned Article?
A commissioned article—one where the publisher (or its editor) asks you to write a piece about a specific topic—can fall under the category of a work made for hire.

A "work made for hire" is a legal fiction which assumes that the person commissioning the work is the author and copyright owner. When you do an article which is viewed as a work made for hire, you have sold all rights, and own nothing more. You may not even reprint the article in an anthology of your own work for a different publisher without permission of the publisher to whom you sold your "work made for hire."

Why? A work made for hire is like a work made by an employee for an employer. The publisher's skill arguably goes into the topic selection, the shaping of the article, and the like, and the publisher is entitled to all rights.

How do you know if your work is a "work made for hire"? Because you sign a brief agreement to that effect. That is, the new copyright law is very clear that the piece is a "work made for hire" and the words "work made for hire" must be used.

Some publishers are now sending their regular freelancers what amount to form letters stating "all work you do for us now will be viewed as works made for hire." Is this binding? Possibly not, because the law specifies that both publisher and author must sign the agreement. To date, the issue hasn't been litigated. The other tricky issue? What if you get a check which is stamped on the back with words to this effect: "By endorsing this check, the Author agrees that he/she has sold a work made for hire, and has agreed to release all further rights in the work." In a sense, if you endorse, both parties have signed the agreement, with the publisher's signature appearing on the front of the check. While this point has never been litigated to an outcome under the new law, it is possible that simply crossing out the "agreement" and endorsing the check will eliminate the problem, and this has been done by some writers with success, as the bank will usually process the check, and the cancelled check won't be sent to the editor or publisher, but to an accounting department, unnoticed by the publisher powers that be.

Who Owns the Copyright in Articles I Write as Part of My Employment?

Your employer. Your articles are viewed as "works made for hire."

Elsewhere, as we have discussed, "works made for hire" agreements must be made in writing, signed by the author and the purchaser. THIS IS NOT THE CASE WHERE YOU ARE

EMPLOYED BY THE COMPANY THAT PUBLISHES YOUR WORK.

If you are an employee in the usual sense of the term, your employer is even considered the *author* of your work for purposes of copyright registration.

When is the situation not so clearcut? If you sometimes freelance for your employer, but sometimes have a salary. Or, if you are given an office and the use of a typewriter, but are only paid on a "per article" basis. In these grayer areas, it is always a good idea to have a brief statement in writing from your publisher or other employer indicating who is to own what rights. Otherwise, you may find yourself liable for copyright infringement by including *your own* writing in your future works, or you may be surprised to find that your employer—not you—owns the movie rights to the long article you slaved over!

I just sold an article to a magazine and the editors cut and changed it to the point where I am embarrassed to have my name on it. Do I have any rights?

Yes and no.

European countries have long recognized this problem, and have laws acknowledging the "moral right," that is, the right of one who has created a work, to have it free from mutilation by its purchaser, or subsequent purchasers.

Our laws do not recognize the "moral right" as such. However, there have been several court case precedents in recent years suggesting a trend toward recognizing the "moral right" under certain extreme circumstances.

Otto Preminger won such a suit when one of his motion pictures was "seriously injured"—cut and edited in the extreme. Terry Gilliam, writer of the television show "Monty Python's Flying Circus," won another case here in the United States because, quite early on, his work was seriously butchered by a network.

These precedents have some things in common. The creators of the works in question were already well-known for their success with similar works, so that the possibility of damage to their careers was more real than speculative.

Accordingly, a new author is not likely to be given protection analogous to the moral right, while an established author might be.

It is occasionally possible to enter an agreement with a publisher that you have the right to okay or veto editorial changes in your work, but, realistically, unless you are a very hot property indeed, most publishers don't care to bind themselves in this way.

What Are Some of the Points My Lawyer or Literary Agent Will Be Looking for in My Book Publishing Contract?

Virtually all book publishers use some kind of standard, printed contract. Many publishers have updated their contracts to make them less "one-sided," and more attuned to writers' rights. However, some standard pitfalls remain in some contracts, and your lawyer or agent will be looking for the following:

1. *Who owns the copyright?* It is *always* preferable to own the copyright in your own work. With fiction, the publisher generally expects the author to own her own copyright. But with respect to certain nonfiction works, especially textbooks or treatises, some publishers take advantage of the writer's "publish or perish" anxieties to try to own the copyright.

2. *The publisher must publish the work or turn the rights back to the author.* Your contract should include a provision requiring the publisher to publish the work within a certain time period—12 months is usually viewed as reasonable, after which the author has the right to terminate the contract and find another publisher. There is no practical way to force a publisher to publish your book. The next best thing is to make sure you can get the rights back to your own book if the publisher does *not* publish the book within a certain, specified time. That is, unless your contract permits you to terminate for failure of the publisher to publish, you are still

barred from selling that work to another publisher. For example, let's say you have written a textbook—on the aesthetics of roller disco—and have entered into a contract with a publisher, who realizes that the market is flooded with such books, and decides not to come out with yours. Everything has gone smoothly, you've been paid your advance, your manuscript was delivered on time, but you suspect your publisher is waiting until the year 2000 to publish your work as a nostalgic look at 1979. All of a sudden, another publisher calls and says they'd love to publish your book. Can you sell it? Yes, *if* your contract includes a provision of the type we've discussed. Otherwise, *no.*

3. *How much is the advance, and can I keep it if the book isn't published?* An "advance" is just that—an advance against your future royalties. While a first-time author won't have much luck trying to negotiate for a higher royalty rate, s/he may well be able to negotiate for a higher *advance* on royalties. Publishers are more reasonable about increasing the advance payment if they understand you will have to make sizeable out-of-pocket expenses for travel, research, and the like in connection with the book. (Some writers are able to have the publisher agree to expend a certain amount toward such preliminaries.)

How much can you keep if the publisher decides your manuscript is not satisfactory? This depends upon the wording of your contract. Often, an advance under $5,000 will be payable to the author by "halves," ½ upon signing of the contract, and the next ½ upon timely delivery of a *satisfactory* manuscript. Larger advances are payable in thirds, or even fourths. Sometimes the first payment is larger than the rest. Some contracts provide that at least some of the advance is "nonrefundable." That is, come what may, you don't pay it back. Try to have your contract negotiated so that you are never in a position of paying money *back* unless you completely default in delivery of the manuscript. That is, limit the publisher's financial clout so that, should your timely-delivered manuscript be unsatisfactory, the final payment need not be made to you, but you need not reimburse your publisher.

Make sure that your contract explains what happens to monies "advanced from royalties" that your publishers makes for illustrations, indexes, or the like in case the contract is terminated. That is, sometimes a publisher will agree to write the check for a large expense involved in your book—say, paying for a technical illustrator—with the sum to be considered an additional advance on your royalties. If you or the publisher should terminate the contract for one of the reasons permitted by the contract, make sure you and your publisher have agreed as to what happens to the drawings, and that you are not liable for repayment of the illustration expenses.

4. *Indemnification and "Hold Harmless" clauses:* Virtually every contract provides for some kind of representation that the author has not infringed the copyright of another, that the manuscript is not libelous, pornographic, and the like.

These representattions are backed up by clauses making the author responsible for payment of the publisher's legal fees, money damages, and other costs should trouble arise. It is most important to have your attorney negotiate to limit your liability. You should not have to be responsible for payment of the publisher's lawyer from the moment a spurious accusation letter is sent to your publisher.

As to pornography, *you* don't control the places your book will be sold—your publisher does. And as pornography is defined differently in different areas of the country, it is your publisher's decision where to sell your work which is likely to result in trouble. Accordingly, it would not be fair to require you to foot the bill for your publisher's legal bills in this regard.

Similarly, because your publisher is, or should be, acquainted with the libel laws, and has chosen to publish your manuscript, he or she should share in the risk of a dispute based on libel. It would be reasonable for you to indemnify your publisher for your negligence in not researching your facts, or for your deliberate libels. But your publisher had the option of having questionable material edited from your manuscript, and, if s/he did not exercise that option, it is not your fault.

As to copyright infringement, it is harder to convince a publisher that s/he should share in the responsibility. However, copyright complaints are occasionally made in situations where an author did *not* copy. To some extent, such "nuisance" claims are a business risk the publisher should share. It is sometimes possible to negotiate a contract to limit your liability to the amount of your advance, for example, or, at your option, to the amount of future royalties, so that you are not stuck with a bill for $50,000 for your publisher's legal fees on a book that earned you $9,000.

5. *Rights and permissions:* Related to indemnification, this clause deals with whether you—or your publisher—is responsible for securing written notice from authors whose work will be quoted in your book.

Ideally, this should be handled by the publisher, at the publisher's sole expense, with the publisher bearing full responsibility for properly securing all rights and permissions. The worst possible contract has the author undertaking the work of contacting the quoted authors, with the author being responsible for paying the authors for their permission. Generally, a first-time author can negotiate at least a compromise between the two extremes.

6. *Revisions of subsequent editions:* Particularly if your book is a nonfiction text, revised editions may be necessary. In this case, your lawyer will want to make sure that *you* have the right to prepare the revised editions, and that you are paid fairly for your work. Many standard contracts provide that if you do not prepare the revised editions at a time, and in a manner, acceptable to the publisher, the publisher has the right to hire another writer to do so. Worse, these contracts provide that the monies paid by the publisher to the other writer will be subtracted from your future royalties. It is possible to revise such a contract so that you alone will pre-

pare revised editions, and it is possible to make sure that you will receive an advance payment for your revision work. Incidentally, the publisher will sometimes try to have your revision advance limited to the amount of the initial advance on the first, unrevised edition. If your book is popular enough to be revised, and, most likely, sold at a higher cover price, you should receive a larger advance than you did at the time the success of the book was not known.

7. *Your right to write:* Many contracts have a provision whereby you are asked to agree not to write and sell other manuscripts on the same topic as your book. Some contracts modify this provision by stating that you are prohibited from writing other books and articles "which may interfere with sales of" the book under contract. Such modifications are often not strong enough to protect you. If you are in a "publish or perish" situation, or are known as an authority in a certain field, you certainly do not want to restrict your right to publish other manuscripts, and your lawyer or agent should be able to delete, or limit, such provisions before you sign the publishing contract.

8. *Option to publish:* Many authors get excited when they see clauses in their publishing contracts indicating that the publisher has an option to publish the author's next book. *Beware!* This does not in any way help the author to have his or her next book published. It is strictly to the benefit of the publisher, and can harm the author. What the provision means is that the publisher has the right to keep you from finding a better publisher for your next book, from negotiating with a new publisher for higher royalties, a bigger advance, and the like. If your publisher hasn't made much effort to promote your book, you don't want to be stuck with that publisher on your next book.

How are such contractual provisions sometimes modified to everyone's satisfaction? You may contract to give the publisher a "first right of refusal" competitive with terms you've been offered by another publisher. That is, you'll be entitled to submit your next manuscript to other publishers, and if one of them offers you a better deal than your present publisher, your present publisher is obligated to match that deal with respect to your second book. If he or she does *not* offer the same deal, then you're entitled to enter a contract with that second publisher.

9. *Royalties not to be held to bail out publisher:* Some contracts provide that, should you have more than one book with the same publisher, the publisher has the right to withhold royalties on your successful work(s) to pay itself back for any losses it sustained with respect to your less successful work(s). This is absolutely unfair to the author, because the publisher is the one who made the business decision to purchase the unsuccessful work, and must bear the risk. Your lawyer or agent should eliminate contractual provisions requiring your subsidization of your less successful works.

These and other pitfalls can often be eliminated, or modified, from the publishing contract your publisher has submitted to you for signature. *When?* Before you sign the contract! That is, such modifications must be made before the contract is "executed," because the publisher has no obligation whatsoever to modify the contract after you've sent him or her your signed agreement!

— Jane Shay Lynch

An Agent Looks at Publishing the "New Author"

Several years ago, Northwestern University acquired the collected business letters of J. B. Pinker & Sons. The Pinker firm was one of the first British literary agencies and achieved enormous success for its clients. The career of the firm spanned over forty years, ending shortly before World War II, when one of the Pinkers entered Sing Sing for absconding with his client's funds.

The Pinkers' list of clients reads like a WHO'S WHO of both England and the United States and includes James Joyce, H. G. Wells, Joseph Conrad, Galsworthy, and numerous other authors.

In addition to their significance for literary research, these letters offer an amusing dêja vu to an agent and attorney who represents writers. Each author's letter and each response echo my daily conversations. Authors' concerns have not changed one whit over the years: "Why didn't you get me a bigger advance? Why isn't the publisher keeping my book in print? Of course the book didn't sell, they didn't advertise it. How can the book sell when I walk into my local book shop and even they don't have a copy." As authors attain fame and financial reward for their efforts, these issues diminish. Then, as now, most of the agent's effort is concerned with the new and lesser known author.

The lesson of the Pinker letters illustrates that, for writers, almost nothing has changed. For the new author, the goal is really very simple—find a publisher and get the book in circulation. Once that's achieved, fame and fortune are sure to follow. What actually follows is not the author's fantasy but the reality of the book world and the book business.

In distinct counterpoint to the lack of change in authors' concerns are the changes in the publishing industry. Although the Pinkers would no doubt adapt, they would no longer recognize the book business or the publishing industry. Similarly, the changes in agenting have become enormous. Even within the last fifteen years, which covers my involvement with writers, the changes stretch the limits of credulity.

It seems appropriate to say that much of the discussion which follows may sound like a defense of the publishing industry. In part, that is true. More germane for both author and editor is one of the rules of negotiating—know thy industry. The book business has become so complicated and multi-layered that you cannot negotiate without a clear understanding of the publisher's problems and the issues that affect his business. All publishers and editors I've met are aware of the issues that affect writers. The difference is in how they manifest that awareness and their success in achieving mutual goals.

Thus, what ought to be negotiated by the agent who is mindful of the mutual needs of author and publisher is not the "best deal" or even the "big deal," but the *fair deal*. The best and the biggest deals are only for the famous and Hollywood. For most of my clients the commitment must be to career development—from which financial rewards can ultimately follow.

As everyone knows, most of the major publishing houses are now parts of conglomerates which specialize in entertainment or "leisure time" industries. As a result, they are subject to the pressures of big and really big business. On the other hand, the people who run the publishing companies do not fit the role of the grey flannel suit corporate executive. In fact, they are people of words, people who love words. They love writing and enjoy publishing; they are anxious to find new authors. However, at the end of each year, their jobs, their incomes, in fact their very businesses, depend upon earning a profit.

The Pinkers would recognize one of the first changes in publishing. They were responsible for it—the agenting process itself. I always tell my clients, especially authors of first books, that in the final analysis I can usually only guarantee them one thing, which is both a blessing and a curse. What I can guarantee authors is a fair reading of their manuscripts by a person at a publishing company who is in a position to make a decision.

Publishers have come to prefer submissions from agents. The agent relieves them of the very time-consuming task of preliminary screenings, and a manuscript coming from an agent seems to give the book a certain respectability. Even more important, if the publisher accepts the manuscript they can feel they will be negotiating with an experienced person who has realistic expectations about what is possible. I often hear from writers that their books, when submitted over the transom, are rejected out-of-hand. But the truth is that no book of quality or book that has a potential for commercial success goes unpublished in this country. You may not be able to sell your book, and I may not be able to place it, and other agents may not be able to place it, but if that's the case, you'd better be prepared to swallow a bitter pill. Regardless of your tender loving care and your years of work, the book may either not be of the quality to justify its publication or may not offer the publisher at least a chance of breaking even.

Yet, some books submitted cold by authors do get published. I'm aware of a recent book that arrived over the transom at a major publishing house after having received eleven rejection slips. It was read by a new employee just one year out of college who loved the book. She brought the book into the house. The book ended up as No. 2 on the Best Seller List, as a major soft-cover sale, and an enormously successful movie. The author, needless to say, is delighted and the young employee is now an editor at that publishing company.

That story is, of course, unique. It most often doesn't happen that way. Publishers and agents get hundreds of unsolicited manuscripts, and there isn't time to read them all. Some New York agents charge a fee for reading a manuscript, and I can understand why. Time is indeed precious. Other agents find that the time and attention that their writer clients require is so enormous that they can represent only a limited number. Although rejections are commonplace, last year there were over 30,000 new trade titles published in this country. Some authors are in fact getting published.

One of the tricks of getting a book published is recognizing which publisher needs a given book at a given time. Recently I started representing a new author who wrote a spectacular first book, and I was sure that a particular publisher would love it. I owed that publisher a favor from a prior transaction, and I gave that publisher first crack at this novel. To my utter amazement, he rejected the novel. It was rejected because the publisher already had two similar books scheduled for publication at about the time this book would be ready for publication, and felt that this would overload and overtax their resources. I'm happy to report that I placed the book at the very next publisher I tried.

Most publishers and agents do not give reasons for their rejections. It's really too painful. The truth may very well be that it's either not a very good book or not commercially feasible. I've come to suspect that one of the reasons good books are rejected is poor editing. I'm not talking about typos, grammar or syntax. I'm talking about the kind of editing that turns a manuscript into a readily readable work. At most publishing firms today, Max Perkins doesn't exist. The company cannot afford to take three or four months of a person's time to help the new author rearrange, reorganize and rewrite major sections of a book. I've become an advocate of writers' co-ops where writers edit each other's manuscripts. (The purpose of this is really quite obvious.) Though the book may still need editing when it gets to the publishing house, the amount of editing required is diminished. To state an economic fact of the book business, publishing a new author represents a substantial financial investment, and a risky one at that. No agents support themselves on new authors, and very few publishing companies break even on new authors. Therefore, what must be done to aid the publishing process is to close the gap between potential income and expense.

To continue my defense of publishing, let me repeat that regardless of the difficulty and the risk, new work gets published, and quality work gets published regardless of the loss. Editors and publishers are still book people.

I recently met with the editor in chief of one of the country's foremost publishing companies and a prominent man of letters who has been widely published, widely praised, and widely awarded, but whose books have not sold. I inquired about another of the publisher's authors. The other author had four published books, each a gem, according to the critics, but none had sold more than 7,500 copies in hard cover. All but one of the books lost money for the publishing company.

I was curious to know how a publisher really deals with a quality book that probably won't sell. This major figure in publishing paused for a moment and said, quite honestly, "We publish them anyway, but please don't lie to me. I don't want the writer or his agent to tell me that here's a great work of art that will sell 100,000 copies. I know, the agent knows and the writer knows that if the book were to sell 7,500 copies in hardcover, we would consider it a roaring success. I'll budget for my losses, but not for lies." He continued, as openly as could be, that in order to support the limited circulation of a quality book, he was prepared—and had to be in order to stay in business—to sell garbage. It's interesting that this particular publishing house probably has one of the highest quality lists and at the same time, one of the largest collections of garbage, as well as cookbooks, children's books, and textbooks and all the "how-to" books you could imagine. It's these books that enable the publisher to make a commitment to a new author. I expect this situation to continue in the future.

About a year ago, I was in the office of another major editor at a different publishing house, and on her desk sat the point-of-purchase advertising displays for one of the leading pieces of junk published in the last several years. I was flabbergasted that this erudite and sophisticated editor would waste her time with such a work. Before I could speak, she looked up at me and said "Shut your mouth. It pays the rent, pays my salary and lets me do with the rest of my time what I want to do." She's right.

Forty years ago, no respectable publisher would have touched this book. But today respectable publishers not only touch these books, but also go out and search for them, have them commissioned and promote them like crazy. All this is done to the consternation of quality authors who view the publishers with scorn for promoting books like these. In reality, they ought to be grateful, for without the big blockbuster there's no possibility of publishing unknown writers.

Publishers have other redeeming qualities. They commission works, and they "carry authors." Many books are conceived by editors, and, through agents, writers are found to produce them.

Similarly the "right" writer can be paid advances forever while he grinds out the work. It's no secret that twelve years passed between Styron's last book and *Sophie's Choice*. I don't know the substance of Styron's contract, but Random House was his last publisher, and Random House is his publisher now. Somehow, Styron supported himself during that period of time, whether through partial advances, prepublication fees, past royalties or savings. It's also no secret that Joseph Heller jumped from Knopf to Simon & Schuster several years ago because Knopf was unprepared to support him if he took an additional twelve years to write *Good as Gold*. Heller has been quoted in the *New York Times* as saying that he used all of his S & S advances to support himself while writing his new book, and I believe him.

Now that it seems I have totally sold out to the publishers, I want to return to the idea of the fair deal for both the new author and the publisher. In order to place an author's book and negotiate a fair deal, the agent needs a sense of the publisher's business. Books weigh a lot and cost a lot to produce and getting them from the printing plant to the book stores in an orderly way and on time is an extremely difficult and costly task. Take note now, book stores do not buy books for resale from publishing companies; they are put there on consignment. If a book store takes 50 books and six months later returns 40, the publisher is stuck with them. What's more, I've been told, though I do not know first-hand, that in today's market place, the cost of publishing is so high that a typical hard-cover book has to sell about 15,000 copies to break even. Do you remember the last time you saw a hard-cover book for much less than $10.00, or a soft-cover book for less than $2.50? I repeat again that in order to negotiate a fair deal, you have to start with a sense of the possible.

One of my many mistakes illustrates what happens when a fair deal isn't negotiated. I was representing an author who, though established and published, happened to be the author of a book on the "newest" of topics. Three publishers were chasing me for the book and drove the price higher. Two were left in the bidding. When we got down to the last survivor, I proceeded to negotiate the highest possible contract which left the publisher with a bad deal, whereas my client had the best of all possible deals.

The book, though excellent, bombed. The publisher lost a fortune, and my client and I are almost personae non grata with that publishing firm. His next book was published by another house and for a small advance. If you push the publisher to the wall with your book contract and cut a deal too tight, you run the chance of burning your bridges. For most people who write, it's not just the first book but the second and third and tenth that are at issue. A fair deal is one that permits the author his share but gives the publishing company a chance to make money as well. For better or worse, publishers are capitalists, and if they don't see the chance of making a buck, they take their losses and run. I've learned over the years that the author will make more money if the publisher also has a chance to make money. What's more, the publisher can join in the orderly and systematic building of the author's career.

The one-time author who writes of being abandoned in the Andes or has one cookbook under her belt, falls into an entirely different category. When you hear about the "big book deals" unfortunately it is the Haldemans and Nixons that score. With such authors you go for the jugular. Developing a writing career is not the objective for them. With only one book to write, the issues change.

Although some agents support themselves by representing "name" writers, the bulk of our work is with the not-yet-famous. What ought this author expect as he approaches the negotiating process?

First, the author is looking for an advance. Bear in mind that the advance is exactly that. It's an advance against future royalties of the book from whatever source. If the book does not earn its advance, it doesn't mean that the author has to pay it back, but it very well may mean that no future funds will be forthcoming.

Please disregard what you read in the newspapers—the million dollar advances are very rare. They're for Mailers and the like. Even these authors, to my knowledge, don't receive the advances their P.R. agents want you to believe they get, and when they do, it's just a very rare situation. The typical author of a first novel receives a very modest advance. In my experience an author's first advance can range from a low of $500 to a high of $25,000. A unique book that hits a particular publisher at the right moment may get a $25,000 advance. More typically, though, an advance for a first book ranges from $2,500 to $10,000.

In addition, most publishers do not pay an advance in one fell swoop. They pay part of the advance on signing of the contract and the balance on the submission of an acceptable manuscript. Many publishers attempt to pay the balance of the advance on the publication date.

Assuming we get a reasonable advance, which for new authors is almost always the major issue, we find that other questions arise. The first is the author's shares of royalties from hard-cover publication. Until recently, in tradebooks this has traditionally been 10% of the list price for the first 5,000 copies sold; 12½% on the next 5,000 and 15% on all books sold thereafter. These numbers have usually been tied to some adjustments based on the method of distribution used and the discount system employed. Recently, however, several publishing companies have been attempting to pay a straight 10% on the first 15,000 copies sold. They argue, especially with new authors, that the cost of publishing the book and the losses they know they are going to sustain are so high that it's necessary to cut royalties to break even.

An issue that's overlooked by most authors is the "grant of rights." By that I mean, just what is the author selling the publisher? Is it the right to publish the book in the United States only? The United States and Canada? Publish it in English any place in the world? License foreign editions in other languages? For some authors this can be of crucial importance. For most it's of no importance at all, but it's an issue that must be discussed between author and agent.

In terms of the contract, soft cover sales have become the most important issue. The biggest change in publishing in the last several years is the predominance of soft cover sales. Not only have these rights become of major importance to authors, but they are also of crucial importance to the publishing company. The soft-cover resale now makes the difference between profit and loss at most publishing companies. Except for the unique best seller, much of an author's income comes from the resale of a book to a soft-cover house. For the overwhelming majority of authors, no publishing company will make a substantial advance, nor will many even consider publishing the book, unless the author grants the right to re-license a soft-cover sale. Twenty years ago, soft-cover sales were handled by publishers' secretaries. Those secretaries now occupy the corner offices in their suites and in most cases are being paid more than the editors and chiefs and publishers of their companies.

Some authors attempt to retain the right to negotiate the soft-cover sale. For new authors, this turns into disaster. They not only receive less money on the soft-cover resale but they also strip the house of its share of profit. Publishing is a close-knit little world, and the key to a soft-cover sale which can be spectacular, even for a book that does not sell well in hard cover, is knowing where to place the book at a given moment. Most books are virtually auctioned off to soft-cover houses. If Bantam Pocketbooks or Avon happens to have a bad streak for a while, it will be prepared to up the advance enormously to get what it hopes will be a big book for the racks. The rights and permissions people of the major publishing companies who do this work may not know a thing about literature (though many of them really do) but they do know where to look, when and how to move, and they are prepared to work quickly. The rights and permissions people at Random House or Simon & Schuster or Harper & Rowe are in continual communication with the buyers for the soft-cover houses. They work with each other closely, they see each other socially, and it's a very peculiar agent (if any) who can do as good a job for his client as the rights and permissions people at a particular house.

Standard publishing contracts provide that on resale to a soft-cover house, the proceeds are split equally between the publisher and the author. Some publishing houses are absolutely non-negotiable on this point. Others negotiate. I won't go into great detail on how this negotiation goes except to say what you probably already know. If you are a first author, please don't expect a contract identical to Gore Vidal's. If your agent gets too huge a share of the soft-cover pie for you, you'll suffer for it. The publishing house's income as well as the author's comes from the soft-cover rights. If you prevent the publishing company from making its profit, your next book will suffer from it.

Recently, many agents have been selling the author's work to the soft-cover house first. The soft-cover house or the agent finds a hard-cover publisher to take the book for trade publication. Though I've been involved in many such transactions, the only one that proved successful involved an extraordinarily commercial piece of work that was geared to the mass market exclusively. Notwithstanding my distaste for this kind of transaction, it is a trend of publishing in the future. My view is that in the long run, it is detrimental to a writer who claims to be a quality writer. What's more, if the soft-cover house is unable to induce a hard-cover house to publish the book, there is absolutely no possibility of any library sales or any significant shelf life for the book.

The most significant battles I've had over the last several years have had to do with soft cover sales, and I expect those battles to continue. The most grievous disappointments I've had have also been with soft-cover houses. One quick story may illustrate the reasons. I negotiated a major resale of a highly successful book. It hit No. 3 or 4 on the New York Times Best Seller List for several weeks running and certainly should have been a highly successful soft-cover book. Notwithstanding the fact that the soft-cover publisher paid an enormous advance, when the time came for the book to hit the racks at the drugstores, supermarkets and airline terminals of this country, it was virtually not to be found. I flew to New York, ranted and raved. What happened was very simple. "My book" was issued by the soft-cover house the same month as it issued another book that had been No. 1 on the Best Seller List for several months. They geared all their energy, all their attention, all their promotional efforts to this big book and simply ignored my client's book. Soft-cover books have shelf lives, just as cornflakes do, and if they don't sell, the distributor yanks them off the shelf and replaces them with another book. The jobbers who distribute these books across the country are just filling racks with products that sell. The trade-off is simple. Soft-cover may produce the biggest advance but no one may read the book, nor will it be reviewed or kept in print.

Most of us who agent books, whether lawyers, accountants or business people by training, are really not literary types. Our experience is not in the area of literature. We happen to be people who like books and who read. With rare exceptions there's no reason to assume that your agent knows much more about literature than you do. What your agent should know is something about the book business and all of its subsidiary rights, including T.V. and the great silver screen. Agents typically charge 10%, though I'm aware that some agents charge more. When they do a "really big deal" which might include a movie, hard-cover and soft-cover deal all wrapped into one, they may charge more. If you're lucky enough to have that happen to you, I don't suspect you'll much care because you'll have so much money that the amount you'll be paying to your agent, which is fully deductible to you anyway, will be almost inconsequential.

Your agent earns his fee in three ways. First, he gets your book read. Second, he negotiates your contract. Third, and this is most important, he marshalls your book through the publishing process. He meets with, speaks to and is in regular communication with your editor, your publisher, the subsidiary rights people, the promotion people. He plies them with liquor and lunches and basically tries to make sure that your book gets more attention within the publishing house than any other agent's book. He creates excitement about your book in the trade. Creating excitement about a book in the publishing house itself can do more to create sales than the quality of the work itself or any other act of promotion. If you represent yourself, you cannot create this excitement. There's no reason to believe, unless perhaps you're writing a book about business, that you know anything about the business of publishing. That's the job that your agent must do. If your editor wants to talk to you about the business side of the book, you may be making a serious mistake. Your editor's only business with you is words: the manuscript, the style, the content, the presentation. Your business is to be the writer, to produce a manuscript that you're proud of and that you believe will sell. Your agent's job is to make sure you get your share of the profits, and a fair deal.

Jerome E. Wexler ©

Performing Arts & the Law

This chapter is addressed to some basic issues and problems which performing artists may face in their careers. For purposes of this chapter, performing artists will include musicians, dancers, actors, and vocalists, as opposed to composers, choreographers, screen and stage writers, and lyricists.

This material will relate primarily to issues arising from performance: contractual relations, rights of personality, protection of style, and financial planning.

Contractual Relations

Contracts are important tools to help plan for and resolve problems, to evidence that agreement has been reached between parties, and to help create good will and trust. Contracts cannot, however, turn bad faith into good or guarantee performance, nor can they be expected to reflect anything other than the respective bargaining strengths of the parties. Performing artists will confront many different types of contracts during their careers, from simple oral agreements to personally appear and perform to complex written recording or management agreements. Whatever the situation performers should be cautious and where necessary seek counsel to help them avoid entering into agreements which may later create problems.

Employment contracts

If you are a member of a performing arts union such as AEA,

AFTRA, SAG, AGVA, or AFM, the terms and conditions of your employment as a performing artist may already be set by negotiations previously carried out between your proposed employer and your union. One point to be made here is the unique position performing artists are in as opposed to members of other types of unions: the terms and conditions set by such a negotiated agreement (or unilaterally promulgated by the union) are *minimums* and you are always free to use whatever bargaining strength you have to obtain better terms from your employer. You may be faced with a "take it or leave it" situation at times, but as your star rises, so of course does your bargaining position.

What happens if an employment agreement is broken? If your employer fails or refuses to allow you to perform, your legal remedies may not be adequate to compensate you for the loss which you feel you have suffered. For example, if a special opportunity to show your talent to a large or influential audience or to participate in a potentially lucrative or fulfilling project is lost, the resultant loss of publicity may be of much greater concern to you than the compensation you were to have been paid for the project or appearance. Trying to obtain compensation for this loss of publicity may be quite difficult, however, since the amount you have been damaged may be so speculative that a court may not permit any compensation to be granted. What to do? Some contracts spell out that a sum of money will be paid to the artist in the event an opportunity for career enhancement is lost. For example, recording agreements often state that in the event the minimum number of recordings called for in the contract are not produced by the record company, the company will pay a sum (usually minimum union scale) to fulfill their obligation. This of course protects the record company more than the artist, but personal appearance contracts may be written with a "liquidated damages" clause stating that, in addition to the compensation lost, a certain sum will be paid to the artist to compensate for the presumed loss of publicity.

If you the artist fail or refuse to appear, what can your

employer do? Your employer may have contractual rights of his own setting forth liquidated damages for his projected loss of profits. Your employer may *not* however force you in a legal proceeding to perform the acts called for in your contract such as to force you to sing or appear on stage. The reasons for this are many, but practically speaking it would be difficult for any court to supervise your performance to insure that you properly comply with its order to perform. An employer *may*, however, prevent you from performing for anyone else until you perform for him, so you could be forced to deal with your former employer after all in order to continue to pursue your career.

Management and agency agreements
At some point in your career you will require an agent to help obtain employment and, perhaps at a later date, a manager to help guide your career. Film and theatre performers generally rely on agents and may, when they have become successful, employ a business manager such as a CPA or an attorney. Talent management consultants have also recently appeared in the film and theatre area to act on behalf of both talent signed under management agreements and producing companies. Dancers have primarily relied on agents rather than managers, while musicians, particularly in popular music, have increasingly turned to managers to handle their affairs.

Managers and agents face two types of regulation: state and union. Most states require agents to register with their respective Departments of Labor or similar agencies and to conduct their business in a specified manner in compliance with various regulations. A few states, in addition, require managers to register. Union regulations usually require that members deal only with agents who have been approved or "franchised" by the union. Agents must apply to the union and agree that their compensation and manner of conducting business will comply with union limits and regulation. To the extent that managers procure employment, they are also required to be union franchised in order for members to deal with them.

Often an agency or management agreement will be offered to talent with the comment that it is a "standard form." While it is true that unions, guilds, employer associations and industry business practices may produce contracts which appear alike, contain similar provisions, or address identical issues, contract terms can vary widely, and one should *never* sign an agreement simply because it appears or is represented to be "standard." When you are offered a contract, that contract actually represents the offeror's policy of how it chooses to do business, what the offeror perceives its bargaining position to be, or the result of negotiations between the offeror and a respective union. Union or guild agreements do become standard in certain recurrent situations, but those agreements are generally *minimum* agreements above which you are free to bargain if you are in a position to.

What does one look for in an agency agreement? Agency fees are usually ten percent of compensation earned from employment obtained by the agent. Agents usually expect to be exclusive, meaning that they do not want to share agency responsiblities and income with anyone else. The expectation is also quite often that the exclusivity will extend to all areas of the entertainment industry. If you prefer different agents for different geographic locations or entertainment areas, this should be spelled out. Agents generally expect to collect the artist's income on the artist's behalf, deduct their compensation, disperse other checks for expenses, and then remit the remainder to the artist. If you are able to handle your own accounts and maintain a stable business address, perhaps you may wish to receive the compensation directly and account to the agent and others instead.

What is the duration of the agency contract? Most terms are for an initial period of one year with several one year options to extend. Perhaps the contract could be structured instead to allow you, the artist, to terminate it if at the end of a period the agent has failed to comply with an objective standard of performance spelled out in the agreement, such as failure to obtain compensation for you greater than an amount agreed to, or failure to obtain employment in a specific industry or location.

How are the agent's expenses handled and what may be charged back against your account without your specific approval? Is the agent asking for an interest in anything other than a percentage share of compensation earned from employment obtained by him or her? If so, such terms should be struck from the agreement. Are you signing an agency agreement because of your special confidence in a particular person with the agency? If so, then you may want the right to terminate the agreement if that person leaves or becomes unavailable to you. Is the agent respected among those with whom he or she will be dealing on your behalf? A simple check with club owners or other clients, for example, may provide you with useful information.

What does one look for in a management agreement? Many of the same issues of exclusivity, control of income and expenses, duration of contract, scope of income participation, and the question of the special personal relationship which arise with agency agreements also arise with managers. The most common and perplexing problem with management agreements however is defining the role managers are to play for their artist clients.

In most cases a performing artist needs his or her greatest assistance in procuring employment. Managers, however, are technically unable to provide this assistance unless they agree to become franchised with the appropriate unions or secure the necessary state licenses. Most managers do not obtain such franchises or licenses because they would not be able to obtain the greatest percentage compensation necessary for them to competently offer the kind of personal and select attention required of a conscientious manager. Agency franchising would limit the managers fee to ten percent, while normal management fees range from fifteen to twenty-five percent. Most performing artists are drawn to managers because they believe that managers will build their careers, which necessarily means obtaining employment. But if an unlicensed manager works directly to obtain employment, then he risks violating the law and acting in a way which may provide a reason for the artist to get out of the management agreement.

In the popular music area, for example, managers are often engaged with the goal of obtaining a recording contract. Securing and negotiating such a contract, however, is an act of procuring employment, and unlicensed managers have in many cases been required in actions brought by formerly managed artists to return money they have received as a part of income earned by such artists from recording agreements obtained by the manager. Most management agreements will state that the manager has not promised to nor will he attempt to obtain employment for the artist, but it is the manager's actions rather than the language of the agreement which will be important.

What does a manager do? Overall, the manager guides and promotes the artist's career by counseling and advising the artist about proper selection and presentation of material, publicity, industry business practices, selection of other professionals such as agents, accountants, and attorneys to assist the artist, and a multitude of other issues that affect the artist's career. The manager plans and protects the best interests of the artist and helps coordinate the many other persons, or entities, who may be using or aiding the artist. Some managers provide financial planning and investment advice, but most prefer to leave this to other professionals to avoid malpractice claims. Managers may also advance money to the artist with the hope that they will be repaid when the artist becomes successful.

Although management fees can be as high as fifty percent of the artist's income, the range is generally between fifteen and twenty five percent. These percentages may be stated in increments, with greater percentages going to the manager at higher income levels, or they may be constant. Managers generally expect to receive a percentage of all income received by the artist in the entertainment area, but this may be limited by the artist if the situation calls for it. For example, musicians may not want their manager to receive a percentage of their income from song-writing royalties or work performed as a producer, arguing that the manager does not have much to do with the earning of that income. In such a case this income could be exempted or the manager could take a lesser percentage. Most managers feel that to "break" an artist in one field makes that artist therefore valuable in others. Thus, for example, the manager of an actor feels that he or she should receive a percentage of that actor's record royalties if he should record, or of a musician's income from a film performance or book. The artist may argue that the manager is competent for one field of entertainment and not others and that other managers may be necessary for those other fields in which the artist may work. In such a case a reduced or eliminated royalty could be negotiated. A manager may also agree to reduce his percentage in the event an agent is hired. This prevents the artist from suffering from reduced income, but it may hurt the manager just when the artist is beginning to achieve success and when the manager expects his or her payoff. A manager may also agree not to take any percentage until the artist achieves a certain income level, but the artist must consider the quality of service he would obtain under such an agreement.

Some management agreements state that the manager will provide services "as and when requested by artist." Such a term should be deleted, since the artist should be able to rely on the continued diligence of the manager to use his or her best efforts in promoting the artist's career. While the manager's services to the artist are not exclusive, they are special, and an artist may be able to negotiate a provision allowing him to terminate the contract if the particular manager is no longer available, or to continue with the approval of the manager's subsequent clients. In addition, artists should not grant any merchandising rights to a manager as part of the management agreement, nor should the manager obtain any interest in the artist's name.

In some instances, particularly in the music area, artists will be asked to sign management agreements together with agreements for the recording of the artist's performances, publishing of the artist's compositions, or some other exploitation of the artist's talent, by companies owned by the manager. There is an obvious conflict of interest in this situation. The manager has a responsibility to the artist to see that the best possible agreements are reached for the artist's services. Will the manager agree to such terms when they apply to his own company? Generally not. Managers are under a greater duty of care to disclose to their artist the terms of any further agreements where there are conflicting interests. Though many careers have been made by such combined ventures, care should be taken before an artist signs a multiple contract. For example, the management contract in such a case should exclude from the manager's commissionable base any income the artist receives from companies owned by the manager to prevent the artist from paying the manager twice.

Recording agreements
Royalties on recording contracts range from five percent to fifteen percent of the retail selling price of a record, and advances on royalties or bonuses for signing range from zero to many millions of dollars. The two best bits of advice to remember regarding recording contracts are (1) don't sign a recording agreement without first obtaining competent legal advice, and (2) don't relinquish publishing rights to your own compositions as part of your recording agreement.

A discussion of the important points to be negotiated in a recording agreement would comprise a book. Generally, however, a recording contract must be viewed from a career planning perspective. To become a successful recording artist may take several releases and careful and persistent work. Large advances may not always be as important as other commitments which might be obtained from a record company which may be more important in guaranteeing your career longevity. Is your act, for example, one that needs strong touring to break your record? If so, a commitment of tour support may be very important. How many records will the company commit to releasing? If only a couple of singles, then you may not have much of an opportunity to prove yourself. What producers will you be able to work with and at what budget? What happens if your records go out of print? Can you release them then yourself? Will prematurely relegating your records to the bargain bins hurt your image? What happens to unreleased recordings after you have left the company? Are you able to perform as a sideman on other recordings? While financial issues are critical in any recording agreement, to lose sight of other career development issues is to threaten the longevity of your career.

Recording agreements are usually for your exclusive services as a performer, and a company will expect to obtain rights to cast albums, sight and sound devices, in addition to regularly recorded records. The term will be for one year with several one year options, and during each term the company will agree to record a certain minimum number of performances with the right to record additional songs at their option. It is important for artists to obtain the company's agreement to release these recordings, although most companies will balk at making specific promises on how they will promote or sell a record upon release.

As more and more self-contained recording artists appear, it becomes more important to maintain some degree of artistic control with regard to compositions recorded, their sequence, album artwork, "A" and "B" sides for singles and the like, both during and after the term of the contract. Companies have different policies regarding these matters, but if some control is not available to you after you have left one company for another, you may find your new material competing with hastily repackaged material previously released or material that was never released at all.

The costs of recording are almost always recoupable by the record company against royalties earned by the artist. Thus if a record cost $150,000 to record, and the artist received about $ .75 per record album sold for a royalty, that artist would be required to sell 200,000 albums before he or she recieved any money. Other costs are often recoupable, such as advances, tour support, some producer's fees and sometimes special promotions. It is not unusual at all for a recording act to remain indebted to the record company through several releases until a later success recoups the prior costs. Although an artist may leave a label in an unrecouped position, companies seldom, if ever, pursue the artist for the unrecouped difference.

The process by which an artist obtains a record contract is filled with pitfalls. A warning must be given not to deal with any company which asks you to pay for its services to record your performance and then promote these recordings through test market releases and other such ventures, with the hope that major label distributors will become interested in the record and pick it up for distribution. For the amount that you spend for these so-called services you can usually produce a quality demo yourself, and the legitimacy or value of the test-marketing services, if they exist at all, has yet to be demonstrated.

When a performer does not have enough money to pay for the recording of a demo, a studio may often offer the use of its facilities at a reduced rate or at no cost to the performer in return for a percentage of any recording contract which may result from the demos recorded. If such an agreement is properly drawn, an artist may benefit from such an arrangement. Without counsel, however, the percentage may be unreasonably high or apply too broadly for the actual value that the studio has given to the artist, and later conflicts may arise about money owed if a recording contract is obtained, whether the demos had anything to do with the contract or not. Also the ownership of tapes recorded under such conditions may be uncertain, and the artist may see such tapes later released without permission to exploit his or her subsequent success. All of which to the detriment of the artist.

It should be noted that recording artists may soon acquire a new right which could result in significant additional income for them. Just as song composers now have the right to receive compensation whenever their song is performed, recording artists may soon have an analogous right to compensation every time a recording on which they perform is played. This royalty is to be distinguished from the royalty they now earn when the recording is sold. Performance royalties for recording artists have been debated for some time. A provision for such a right failed to be included in the new copyright act, but bills to amend the act and create such a right are now pending. If such a royalty is created, compensation would be divided between the artist and the record company releasing the record. Although information about the amount of compensation to be expected and the process by which it will be collected must await passage of an actual bill, such passage appears more likely now than at any prior time. In the meantime, all recording contracts should contain a provision addressing this right and providing for how performance income will be divided if it is obtained.

Rights Agreements
Performing artists often perform material which they have created. In such cases there is little need to worry about rights agreements unless the performer has assigned his or her rights to the performed material to someone such as a producer or a production or a publishing company.

When a performer wishes to use the work of another, however, it must be used only with the permission of the owner of the work or by taking advantage of an exemption which exists in the copyright laws. As explained elsewhere in this book, the owner of a copyright in a literary, musical, dramatic, or choreographic work, pantomime, motion picture, or other audio-visual work has the exclusive right to perform such work and to authorize others to do so. Moreover, the copyright owner of a work has the exclusive right to prepare derivative works based upon the original copyrighted work. The owner of a short story or novel, for example, has the exclusive right to authorize movies, dances or songs to be prepared based upon this work, as does the owner of a song with a story narrative content such as "Tom Dooley" or "Ode to Billie Joe" or a thematic album such as *Sgt. Pepper's Lonely Heart's Club Band* or *Desperado*.

How does one locate a copyright holder? Many popular theatrical or musical stock rights are handled by agencies such as *Tams-Whitmark* or Samuel French. These rights are fairly easy to obtain. It is important to note that obtaining rights does not confer permission to change or adapt the work. The holder of stock rights is entitled only to present the work as prepared and licensed. Changing a work without further permission would violate not only copyright laws but also the provisions of most stock licensing agreements. To adapt a work from one medium to another may take more investigative effort. Publishers are generally the best place to start, since they will either have the rights you wish to acquire or know where the author may be reached. If that effort fails, the Copyright Office with the Library of Congress will conduct a search of its files for an hourly fee, which is quite reasonable. Locating the proper copyright holder may at times prove frustrating, for it is not uncommon to discover competing copyright claimants to the work which you wish to adapt. Unless you persuade the competing owners to settle or obtain rights from both, you risk lawsuits from either of them if you proceed with the permission of only one. On the other hand, you may find that the work is in the public domain, in which case no rights agreement would be necessary.

Once you have located the proper owner, an option or rights agreement may then be negotiated if the rights are available. The terms and provisions of these agreements are explained in the chapter on film. In this chapter we will discuss some additional issues which pertain particularly to performers.

Composers of musical compositions have the right to be compensated any time that their song is performed. Performance means not only a live performance, but also playing a record featuring a performance, broadcasting a live or recorded performance, or rebroadcasting such a broadcasted performance. Performance does not include synchronizing the song with a film or television image to produce a soundtrack, use of a song in commercials or for other purposes of trade or use in connection with theatrical or dramatic performances. Almost all music composers assign their right to performance royalties to either ASCAP (American Society of Composers, Authors and Publishers) or BMI (Broadcast Music, Inc.) to enforce for them. ASCAP and BMI in turn grant blanket licenses to all users of music to allow such users to perform or use the music contained in the complete ASCAP and BMI catalogs. Licensees include television and radio stations, nightclubs, discos, performing halls, universities, restaurants, sports stadiums and others. The license fees are generally based on the advertising or ticket revenues of the licensee. The license fees collected are disbursed to composers and publishers by ASCAP and BMI according to the number of performances of each composition which ASCAP or BMI record in their logs.

If a performer chooses to include in his or her repertoire a song composed by someone else, that performer generally is not required to obtain permission from the composer since theoretically the composer is being compensated by receiving a portion of the license fee paid by the place in which the performer is performing the song. If you perform "Yesterday" in a piano-bar for example, John Lennon and Paul McCartny theoretically receive their share of the bar owner's license fee in compensation. If you include "Yesterday" in a film however, or a stage play or as background music for a commercial, you must obtain a proper license.

In the past there was some uncertainty about the ability of a choreographer to copyright his or her work. Registrations were made by a few choreographers of their significant work, but there was no specific mention of the law about how choreography was to be registered or protected. That situation changed with the appearance of the new copyright law in 1978. Choreography, if it is recorded in some form, may now be registered and protected the same as any other copyrightable work. Dancers therefore must exercise some greater caution in ascertaining whether the work they are performing is properly authorized.

Performers often take a composition and arrange it to fit their own performing styles or cast the composition in a style identified with them. Jazz musicians, in particular, spontaneously arrange songs for artistic effect. What, if any, are the problems when this occurs? First, the right to make arrangements of a song belongs to the owner of the copyright in the song. Therefore, the performer obtains no rights in any arrangement he may create unless a grant of rights is specifically made by the owner. Such a grant is seldom, if ever, made. When arrangers work with permission of copyright owners, they usually only pay a fee, while the owner retains the copyright in the underlying song and the copyright to the arrangement also. Is an arrangement an infringement? Technically it may be, for it could be deemed a derivative work prepared without authorization. Practically, the owner of a song will not pursue any performer performing a new arrangement of it unless that performer is claiming or receiving compensation for the arrangement. The owner will be happy with anything that adds life and value to the composition. If, however, the arrangement in some way disparages the song or uses it in connection with some other composition in a disparaging manner, the owner of the song may threaten legal action. For example, a rock group recently released a record on which it sang the lyrics to the theme from *Gilligan's Island* over the music from Led Zeppelin's song, "Stairway to Heaven." While a typical mechanical license to record would have allowed the group wide latitude to arrange either song for purposes of recording, the pairing was thought to be damaging and the record was withdrawn.

Performances of copyrighted works may not, under certain conditions and circumstances, require a rights agreement. These are:

1. Face-to-face teaching activities. All forms of work are subject to this exemption. It applies, however, only to

teachers, pupils, and guest lecturers and not to outside performers brought into a class. The performance must also take place in a classroom or similar setting.

2. Instructional broadcasting. This exemption applies only to *nondramatic* literary or musical works and does not include dramatic musicals, operas, comedies or films. There are also several other regulations narrowly limiting this exemption within educational institutions.

3. Religious services. This exemption applies only to nondramatic literary or musical works and performance of dramatic-musical works "of a religious nature." The performance must be in a place of religious assembly during a service.

4. Public reception. This exemption applies to public reception of a performance on ordinary sound systems of a type found in the home, such as small radios or systems with four or less speakers. It does not apply to larger commercial systems possibly found in a nightclub or bar which transmit broadcasts which they have received.

5. Agricultural fairs. This exemption covers nondramatic musical works performed by either the government or the nonprofit organization sponsoring the fair.

6. Performance to promote retail sale of records. This exemption allows in-store play where there is no admission charge.

7. Transmissions for the blind and other handicapped persons. Two exemptions allow broadcsts under specified conditions for handicapped people.

8. Performance by non-profit organization. This exemption has been left for last because it causes the greatest misunderstanding and confusion. It was previously believed by many that as long as a performance was presented under the auspices of a nonprofit organization rights agreements were unnecessary. The new copyright law sets forth specific circumstances under which this remains true. First, neither the performer nor the presenter of an unauthorized work may receive any compensation for their efforts, and the works which they may perform are limited to *nondramatic* literary

or musical works. Second, there must be no admission charge or, if there is a charge, the proceeds of the presentation must be used exclusively for educational, religious or charitable purposes. If a charge is made for the performance, however, the owner of the rights to the work to be performed may still object to the performance by filing a timely, proper notice of objection with the presenters. Many educational organizations were surprised to learn of this very limited exemption when licensing organizations such as ASCAP and BMI began demanding licenses for the use of music used during concert series and the like. Some industry and educational umbrella-type organizations have worked out guidelines for the fair use of copyrighted material in educational circumstances, but the law seems clear that in order to perform without possible penalty any work other than nondramatic literary or musical works these strict rules must be adhered to.

Releases

One important contract performing artists often sign is a release. Do not, as a rule, sign a general release. Always question the purpose for which your likeness, name, or biography will be used, and request that this purpose be inserted in the release as a limitation on the use of your likeness, name or biography. The extent to which one might go to question a use may be illustrated by an occurrence involving a couple walking in a park who were approached by a film company with the request that the couple consent to being filmed as they walked. When asked the purpose of the film, the couple was told that it was for an educational documentary. The couple thereupon consented to being filmed. They were later surprised to find that the documentary was about venereal disease, and that the footage which included them was used in a way which cast them in a false light by implying that they had such a disease.

Releases may also be limited in the duration for which your likeness may be used, the type of product or service with which it may be associated, the type of business it may be sold to, the manner in which your likeness may be changed, if at all, (your face on another body, your face or body distorted, etc.), the other individuals with whom your likeness may be used, or any other limitation which you may desire. Releases should also be keyed to the particular job order number on which your photographer is working.

Arbitration

When disputes arise, there are essentially three ways of resolving them: negotiation, litigation or arbitration. Arbitration involves either a labor matter in which your union and/or employer may be involved or a commercial matter between you and someone with whom you are in contract, such as an agent, manager or author.

Arbitration may only be conducted by agreement between the disputing parties. One side may not force the other to arbitrate. This arbitration agreement is usually found in a provision included in a larger agreement between the parties such as a management, agency or rights agreement in the commercial area or in a collective bargaining agreement in the labor area. In commercial contracts, reference is typically made to the American Arbitration Association. The AAA is a national organization promoting the use of arbitration to resolve disputes. The AAA has rules and procedures regarding how arbitrators are to be chosen and the arbitration process conducted, and the parties usually agree to conduct the arbitration proceedings accordingly. Other agreements may ignore the AAA and spell out the arbitration process which the parties feel is more appropriate for them. Some guild agreements, such as the Dramatists' Guild, specify arbitration according to guild rules. Arbitration may be used for all disputes which arise between parties or only for disputes involving selected issues. Labor arbitration is sometimes conducted by representatives of management and labor. In the performing arts, however, unions will usually insist on conducting arbitration by themselves according to their own rules.

Should you agree to arbitration? Often this is a decision,

which, like many, should be made on advice of counsel. Arbitration may be quicker and less expensive than litigation. Your dispute may be heard by one experienced and familiar with your area of work as opposed to a judge who is otherwise quite competent but who may not be familiar with industry practices.

It is also possible to specify where the arbitration is to be conducted, which may provide you with assurance that you will not have to defend or pursue a claim long distance. On the other hand, arbitration may not afford you the same procedural and legal rights and remedies available with litigation. Arbitration awards are not appealable, for example, and if a losing party fails to comply with an arbitration order, it may be necessary to commence litigation anyway. With regard to labor arbitration, you accept arbitration when you join the union just as you are expected to accept all other rules. Unions will, however, waive the arbitration requirements in some cases where good reason is shown. The point of including this information here is not to equip you to make a seasoned judgment about arbitration, but to alert you to its possible presence in an agreement you may be offered.

Performers Rights

Creative artists are able to rely on the copyright laws to protect their rights from infringement. Performing artists, however, cannot, for some of the works that they create, *i.e.,* their public personality, name, likeness and style—all intangibles which copyright does not protect. These intangibles may be protected, however, and it is important for performing artists to understand how this works.

Personality

For the purposes here, personality refers to the assembled facts, goings on, and views of a performing artist.

The right to protect one's personality arises out of the right which we all have to be left alone: the right of privacy. When a performing artist submits himself or herself to public scrutiny to be either acclaimed or rejected, that artist does not lose that right of privacy. The right, however, does change, and the performing artist will find that certain aspects of the right are lost while others are expanded.

For example, when a person, through either concerted effort or the happenstance of unexpectantly being included in a public spectacle such as an accident or crime, becomes "newsworthy" and thus a public figure, that person then loses some rights to prevent his or her likeness from being used or certain information about their lives to be made public. A well known performer may not stop his or her picture from being taken and printed in the newspaper, for example, because the goings on of that person are items of legitimate concern to the public. The performer may prevent a photographer from unreasonably intruding on his or her seclusion to take a picture, and a picture may not be used in such a way that the performer is cast in a false light, but otherwise the performer's likeness may be used for purposes other than trade without the consent of or compensation to the performer. Facts about the performer's life may also be printed and distributed, but disclosure of embarrassing facts about a performer's private life which are unrelated to the performer's public life, and therefore not of legitimate concern to the public, may be actionable. The more well known a performer becomes, the fewer aspects of their lives remain private and immune from public disclosure.

The above discussion pertains to use of a performer's name, likeness or biography for purposes of news gathering and telling only. Use of these aspects of a performer's life for purposes of trade such as in advertising, on novelties and in connection with other forms of endorsement become more valuable and protectable as the performer becomes more well known.

It is a violation of the law for anyone's name or likeness to be used in an advertisement without their consent. Celebrities' endorsements are usually more sought after than endorsements from unknowns, but all of us enjoy the same protection of the law. Advertisers have recognized that this protection exists and therefore few unauthorized endorsements occur today. Serious problems do occur, however, when names and likenesses are used on unauthorized posters, novelties, tee-shirts, and other items. These bootleg industries, capitalizing particularly on music performers, have grown tremendously in recent years, and performers have had difficulty in stopping them. Legal remedies are available, but they have not been effective in preventing the bootlegging from occuring, usually because the actual bootleggers have been difficult to identify.

Names

Names are protected primarily under concepts of trademark law. Trademarks identify source. If you see "Coke" on a can, you are being assured that the cola beverage in the can was manufactured by a certain company. If you see "Century 21" on a sign, you are being assured the realty services which you will be provided by that firm will be of a certain type. Trademarks arose from the practice of artisans stamping a mark on their work identifying them to be "from the studio of . . . " They make advertising and good will possible, and they also help us trace the origins of defective goods.

Performers often adopt names or titles other than their own under which they perform. Investigating prior use of a name may be difficult for performing artists since unions may not have information about performers other than local members, and performing artists have traditionally not registered names or been listed in the types of directories in which a commercial search firm would look. Some investigation should be made, however, to help avoid a later conflict.

Actually trademark protection begins after a mark has been used, so it is not possible to protect a name you have created prior to disclosing it to the public. After the mark has been used, federal trademark registration, the preferred method of protection, may be undertaken. If federal registration is not possible, state registration may be. If neither are available, it may still be possible to protect the name if it is used long enough and becomes associated in the public's mind with a certain performer. Protection extends to not only preventing other performers from using the name, but also use of the name in other areas, such as on tee-shirts, etc. Trademark protection is also important for any identifying logo, emblem or insignia which the performer has adopted in connection with his performance.

If you do not register the name under which you are performing, or if you perform under your own personal name, do you still have the right to stop others from using the name? Under certain circumstances, yes. Remember that name protection arises only from use. If the use of a name has occurred over a period of time or with such pervasive impact that to hear the name generally brings a certain work or performer to mind, then that name is said to have developed secondary meaning. *Gone With The Wind* may or may not be registered, but the title cannot be used without being associated with a particular book or movie. When secondary meaning develops in a name or title, that name or title may defeat even a prior use of that name if the right to use the name or title is ever contested. For example, the makers of the film *Exodus* were able to prevent an earlier film of the same title from being shown under that name. The public was better acquainted with the book from which the second movie was adapted, and would thus tend to be confused as to the origin of the first movie. In some cases people with names identical or similar to names of more famous performers have been prevented from using their own names even in businesses unassociated with the performing arts. Therefore, the more famous you become, the greater protection you have in your name.

Another problem involving names which may be prevented is called passing off. Even if you may not have developed secondary meaning sufficient for protection, if another act is using your name to pass itself off as you or your act, you may stop that use. Whether passing off has occurred will depend on the circumstances. If your name is a common one, it may be necessary to show that the use is part of a scheme to deceive the public and capitalize on your efforts. If your name is more distinctive, you will have a lesser burden of proof.

Protecting a name may also involve stopping former group members from performing under the name either while you want to continue using it or after you have gone on to other projects. The best solution to this problem is preventive: decide early by contract what happens to a group name in the event the group dissolves. If no such agreement exists, a court may look at several considerations to decide who owns the name. Was the name previously used by one member? If so, that member may have a greater claim to it. Is the name the property of the business entity under which the group conducted business? If so, it is an asset to be distributed when the entity dissolves. For example, the group Rare Earth operated as a corporation and the group's name was a corporate asset. When the group dissolved, the owners of the greatest percentage of stock in the corporation were allowed to continue using the name. Will continued use of the name after a principal member or members have left confuse the public as to the makeup of the old group or unfairly compete with the subsequent careers of the members who leave? If so, perhaps the name may only be used in connection with the original group lineup and no others. Stephen Stills and Neil Young, for example, successfully prevented the drummer for their former group, the Buffalo Springfield, from using the name after they had left the group to pursue solo careers.

Right of publicity

While it is clear that the unauthorized use of the actual name, likeness or voice of another is preventable, it is less clear that imitation or derivative use of the same may also be stopped.

Borrowing by performers of another performer's voice or style is not often done except in imitation or burlesque. Although all performers borrow from other performers, each knows that he or she must be unique in order to be successful. As in the case of names, a performer may be prevented from passing himself off as another, but theft of style for that performer's own purposes may be more difficult to prove to stop. Parody and burlesque enjoy a greater freedom to borrow, since it is necessary to conjure up the original performer in order for the parody to be successful. Parody as a way of commenting upon or criticizing performers also enjoys some protection as a necessary form of expression. The parody, however, may be only for a limited use in order for it to be considered a fair use. Parody may also be so strong, or an imitation done so poorly, that it may constitute a defamation of the performer. Short of passing off or wrongful parody, however, performers will have difficulty preventing other performers from borrowing from them. If a performer, after all, could "wrap up" a vocal or visual style, growth in the performing arts might end, since no one would dare to apply their own talents to aspects borrowed from another without fear of a lawsuit.

Advertisers often imitate performers in their ads, many times after they were unable to come to terms with the original performer being mimicked. This imitation may or may not be preventable, depending on the circumstances. First, this type of commercial use cannot be defended as parody, for the near likeness—style or voice—is used for purposes of trade and not as comment. There are also factual questions about whether an imitation has actually occurred. The more distinctive the likeness or vocal or visual style of a performer, the more likely it is that the performer will be able to prove that a wrong has occurred. There is also a question whether a performer is the proper person to bring an infringement suit. The right to prevent unauthorized uses of likenesses of vocal or visual styles has been personal with the performer. It may occur that the performer achieves his or her greatest acclaim in a character role for which the performer has created certain effects. If rights to the character belong to someone other than the performer and it is aspects of the *character* which are being borrowed, it is not clear whether the performer has the right to prevent an imitation.

The direction of the law today is to view the right of

publicity as a *property right* which a performer may develop during his or her lifetime. The right is not a complete or absolute right, but must be nurtured and protected in order for it to come into being. This development is very significant. If the right is a property right rather than a personal right, then infringement actions will be easier to maintain. Performers may more easily assign the right to others during their lifetime to exploit. And, most important, the right survives the death of the performer. In the case of such performers as Elvis Presley, the survival of this right to prevent unauthorized uses of a name or likeness is worth millions of dollars. If, however, the performer fails to nurture this right of publicity during his or her lifetime, it may terminate at the performer's death.

Financial Planning
Guidance in the area of recordkeeping and taxes is provided elsewhere in this book. Financial planning is a necessary second step which refers to techniques which may be used to reduce the amount of taxes you might otherwise be required to pay as well as to preserve and protect your capital.

Planning generally involves deferring the recognition of income to a time when the taxpayer will be in a lower tax bracket or when the income may be of greater value. Deferral may be accomplished by means of careful contract negotiation, retirement programs and tax shelters.

The nature of the performing arts industry leads to great variations in income. A performer may receive a great deal of money bunched into relatively short periods. These periods may occur several times during the performer's career, or only once. The goal of planning is to provide continuity of income to the performer and to prevent taxation at maximum rates in the years high income is earned. Some spreading of income is accomplished by *averaging income* with lower income received in previous years. Other spreading may be accomplished by providing in a contract that income will be paid in increments over several years instead of all at once in one year. The advantages of spreading are that the goals of lower tax rates and income continuity may be achieved, but the artist must realize that he or she must place this future income at risk in order for the deferral to remain valid. If, for instance, the income is placed in a trust which provides for periodic payments and which is controlled by the artist, the artist could be deemed to have received the full amount of the trust corpus at the time of creation. This may result in the tax planning advantages being wiped out. If the artist later finds he or she needs greater amounts than provided for in the agreement and tries to subsequently change the agreement, the tax planning effects might also be threatened. In order for any contractual deferrment to be valid, the deferrment must be arranged *before* the contract is signed. Agreements reached at a later date are not valid. Therefore, consult your advisor prior to completing your transaction. It may be possible in some instances to structure an advance loan instead of royalties which may have the same effect as a deferred payment contract.

One of the best financial planning devices currently available is a pension plan IRA, or Individual Retirement Plans, available for employed performing artists who are not otherwise covered by a qualified pension plan. Keogh plans are available for self-employed performing artists. IRA plans allow you to set aside up to $1,500 pre-tax dollars annually in an account, the interest on which will be tax-free. Keogh plans allow up to $7,500 in contributions under similar circumstances. These sums may not be withdrawn without penalty until the contributor is 59½, when it is presumed that the contributor will be in a lower income tax bracket. Withdrawals will be taxed then at the contributor's then current tax rate. Check with your advisor as to the plan best suited to your own needs.

Performing artists will be presented with many types of tax shelter plans, because of both the nature of the performer's income and the industries in which shelters are offered, such as movie productions, master recordings, book publishing and the like. Most shelters other than oil and gas and real estate have lost their value as anything other than a deferral mechanism due to recent tax reform measures. Unless a performer is likely to earn interest from the retained tax monies which have been deferred, a simple deferral plan may not be of much benefit and may actually cost the performer more in unforeseen penalties and expenses. Shelters currently available in oil and gas and real estate allow taxpayers to deduct from their income amounts greater than the capital amounts contributed to the sheltered venture. The difference between the deduction and the actual contribution represents sheltered income. Tax advantages may also be achieved with properly planned sales of property. It is critically important to discuss with your advisor any participation in a tax shelter venture.

One popular technique for financial planning for performing artists is doing business as a corporation rather than as an individual. The corporate form allows greater profit sharing and pension plan contributions to be made, together with deductible health and life insurance fringe benefits. It has the additional advantages of limited liability, continuity of life, transferability of interests, and a greater potential for financing. Care must be taken, however, to set up and operate the corporation properly to avoid tax penalties and problems which may arise when closely held corporations such as those formed by single performing artists earn most of their income from personal services and royalties. The corporate form of business also necessarily entails greater record keeping and professional assistance. Despite these drawbacks, when a performer begins to earn annual amounts approaching $50,000, incorporation may be desirable.

Performers may acquire income producing properties such as copyrights, interests in shows, films, or stock, during their careers. One method of tax savings is to shift the income earned by these assets to other family members who may be taxed on such income at lesser rates. This is accomplished by transferring the assets to the family members or to a trust set up for their benefit. Such a transfer will comprise a gift subject to gift taxes, but annual exclusions may cause the gifts to pass tax free. Short-term or "Clifford" trusts may also be set up which will allow a gift to revert back to the donor after a ten year period, during which income from the gift is taxed to the donee at rates which could result in substantial tax savings.

Thought should also be given by performing artists to estate planning techniques that could result in tax savings and help insure the integrity of the body of creative work which the artist has created over his or her lifetime. Use of trusts, lifetime gifts, insurance, and other techniques can help insure that your heirs will be able to enjoy the fullest benefit of your estate. If you wish to also insure that your work will be handled in a manner which will maintain its integrity and availability, then you should also provide, through gifts, trusts, and a will, that such work will be left with competent and reliable people under the conditions specified by you.

—Thomas R. Leavens

Film and Video
and the Law

So you want to do a movie, and you've never done one before, either as writer, producer, director, or actor? You have this fantastic idea that no one has ever done before, or at least hasn't done in the specific way, and with the clever twist you have added. And the movie, if it gets made, is going to gross millions and start a whole new trend in movie making.

You begin by talking to friends about your idea, and they either get excited about it, in which case they are truly your friends, or they are somewhat discouraging, in which case they are fair weather friends, and who needs their negativism, anyway. Somewhere along the line, though, someone is going to say to you, as inevitably as death, taxes, and freeloaders, "Well, have you talked to a lawyer about all this?" You may respond, "Of course not; it's too early," or "I can't afford one," or what is most likely, "I don't really know any lawyer who specializes in this area." Well, the more you talk to people, the more you will become convinced that, in the same way that you go to a doctor to check on a suspicious ache or pain, you should go to a lawyer, if only to find out what you might have to worry about later.

So you get a name from someone, or you have a friend who is a lawyer, but anyway, you go. And wow! You thought some of your friends were negative, but never have you heard anything like this. First of all, the lawyer explains that you won't be able to protect your idea as such, so you'd better not keep blabbing it around or it will get stolen and you won't be able to do anything about it. Then you'll be told that it's next to impossible to sell an idea to the movie studios, and you have to know somebody who knows somebody who knows the studio president just to get your script read. Next, you are told that if you want to make the film yourself, you can't sound out friends, relatives, rich acquaintances and the like about sinking money into your venture until you have complied with all sorts of strict laws regarding the raising of money. Even after you have complied, you discover you have to make your venture sound like investing in the building of another Hindenberg without any new safety devices. Finally you are warned that even if you get your movie made, you'll have to give so much of it away to stars, directors, distributors, composers, and assorted other creative types that there may be nothing left for you.

So you say to yourself, "Well, maybe the concept will work just as well for television, if not better, and just maybe, the right medium for this idea is really television, after all. I'll talk to the lawyer about shifting the whole concept and see what he or she says about that." And you find out to your absolute dismay that the advice is not much different, and that no matter how you decide to develop this creative brainstorm of yours, it's going to cost you far more than you ever dreamed, and is going to be much more complicated than it originally seemed.

Finally, in frustration and despair, you cry out to an unsympathetic and polluted night sky, "Why, oh why, can't I just take this creative brainstorm, which I know beyond certainty is worth millions, and just run with it? Why, oh why, does a cruel and relentless society force me to be a businessperson when all I really want to be is a creative artist?" That cry will join the millions of others, identical in thought if not in words, that have gone before it over the centuries. It is probable that Michelangelo, while agonizing over the creation of the Sistine Chapel ceiling, was also agonizing over the commercial compromises he was forced to make to please an unsympathetic patron. It is certainly true that creators/artists over the years have had, at least early in their careers, to cater to commercial considerations at the expense of pure immersion in their art. For whatever comfort it gives, you are not alone.

Why is it that our society makes it so difficult for artists to simply create, for the benefit of untold millions of people contemporary and yet unborn? One of the answers lies in headlines we all see from time to time, and in similar unprinted stories. Those headlines talk about how some famous person, perhaps a movie star or a prominent athlete, was "taken" by a scheme involving a coal mine, or an oil well, or a Broadway play, or some other "sure thing". The history of the United States includes not only the invention of such things as the light bulb and other marvels, but also the exploits of some of the great so-called "con men" who in their time have fleeced millions out of millions.

In an attempt to identify these fleecers as law-breakers, our lawmakers have made it very difficult for anyone to contribute to a scheme to make money unless the person making the promises complies with laws designed to protect the investor. The concept makes great sense outside the arts, because almost by definition, salespeople are talking about commercial ventures designed only to make money (although some greater benefit to mankind may accrue). With the arts, however, commercial success has always been considered by the artists as secondary, albeit vital to the survival of the art form. If a particular work of art succeeds financially, it will encourage other artists to create and at the same time provide the successful artist with sustenance so that he or she can continue creating.

However, one of the serious problems facing anyone who has not yet proven himself or herself in the field in which they choose to labor is trust. Each creative individual who wishes to burst onto a particular scene with something startling, something new, something important, has to overcome the burden imposed by impostors who have appeared over the centuries. The burden is to show somehow that the new person is not a charlatan, a fake, a con artist who is interested less in art and more in taking the money and running. So many have done, and continue to do the latter that there is a tremendous mistrust to overcome. Thus the plethora of laws that have been passed to protect the unwary from the untrustworthy. All of this makes your job that much more difficult because no one knows who you are and why you will not take the money and run, but rather will do with it everything you say you will do. As your attorney has advised you, the laws do not say "Thou shalt not create;" rather, they say "Thou shalt create all thou wishes, but if thou wish to raise money in connection with thy creation, thou shalt obey the law, under penalty of stiff fines and repayments."

So, you say, I may disagree with all of that, or I may agree with it, but in any event I am stuck with it, so let's go on. Let's say for a minute that I decide to forego some of my profits by letting someone else have the headaches of raising the money to do this film or this television pilot (assuming I can sell someone on that), and giving that person a piece of my profit pie. What's this you're telling me about my not being able to protect my idea? Do you mean that anyone can rip me off and I won't be able to do anything about it? What about mailing myself a registered letter with my idea; what about copyrighting it? Isn't there something I can do? I mean, it's ridiculous to think that I can struggle to create something that absolutely anyone can take. What are the copyright laws for anyway?

These are reasonable questions. The answers may not seem to be reasonable, but from a dispassionate, objective viewpoint, they are. Let's start with an overview of copyright laws generally, and from there analyze how they fit this situation.

The United States Constitution provides that Congress shall provide authors and inventors with protection for a limited period of time for the results of their intellectual and inventive labors. Where you see the word "authors," read *creators,* since the term has come to mean in copyright parlance anyone who creates a work that can be copyrighted. What can be copyrighted? The answer in a moment

First, what is a copyright? Essentially, it is a claim of ownership in an exclusive right to copy an original work that has been created intellectually and is not an invention. "Exclusive", of course, means "to the exclusion of everyone else in the world." That definition is an oversimplification, but in essence, it covers the subject. Inventions are covered by patents; literary works, photographs, maps, films, music, and plays are examples of works that can be protected by copyright. To become more basic, we can discuss the three major areas of intellectual property law—patents, copyrights, and trademarks—and distinguish them, and perhaps emerge with a somewhat clearer picture. Patents, as we have noted, cover inventions. Another category of intellectual property law is trademarks, and they indicate the source of a class of goods. Usually, trademarks are names or slogans, rather than complete works of art. They are protected so that people who build up a large amount of goodwill in a product through careful quality control and advertising over the years are not subject to having their good name and reputation destroyed by someone else who uses the same or a confusingly similar name. Trademarks can last forever, if the product they identify lasts forever and the owners take some care to continue the protection.

Thus, for example, your favorite beer (assuming you have a favorite beer) has a name, and you can be confident each time you purchase a can or bottle of that beer that it was bottled under a license from the same distillery that always made that beer. There are exceptions which need not concern us here, such as the purchase of the company that owns the trademark, or the purchase of the trademark itself. The point is that no *unauthorized* use may be made of a protected trademark, and the owner of that mark may protect it for as long as the products that use that name continue to be made and marketed. It is easy to distinguish this protection of names and slogans from copyrights, the intellectual property area that covers a complete individual, creative endeavor such as a story, a book, a movie, a play, a song or a map. All of those works are complete in and of themselves, and copyright protection extends to each of those works individually.

Protection for a work that is copyrighted is limited; that is, it cannot last forever no matter what the owner does. It may not last at all if the owner does not take some elementary steps at the very start, but in any event, for works created after January 1, 1978, protection is afforded for the life of the author plus fifty years. Well, the question might be asked, "How does this keep me from protecting an idea, since my idea was for a movie, and you just said that movies are copyrightable?"

The answer is that copyright protection extends only to the tangible, physical expression of an idea, and not to the idea itself. What's the difference? If you tell me about a great story you intend to write, that story has not yet been reduced to a *tangible, physical* expression and is therefore not protected by copyright law. If you write down your idea, then *that writing* is what is protectable, and in some instances even the subject about which you wrote. To make a complicated subject even more complicated, facts are not protectable by copyright, for the simple reason that as a matter of common sense they ought to be available to everyone. Remember that a copyright owner has a virtual monopoly on the material that is the subject of the copyright. Thus, if facts were protectable, the first person to write about a catastrophe, for example, would be able to thereby exclude the rest of the world from writing anything at all about that event. There arise some questions about what constitutes a fact, so that calling a person's nose too long may be a fact, depending on what a viewer considers too long, but for purposes of this discussion we can avoid such esoterica. Suffice it to say that only where ideas have been reduced to a tangible medium may they be protected by copyright.

Why? Well, for one thing, it is extremely difficult to prove anything about something that exists only in someone's mind. For another thing, there are a number of general ideas for plots that are already in the public domain, unprotected by any copyright, and therefore capable of being utilized with variation by anyone. As an example, let us suppose I want to develop a story that revolves around an ambitious politician who decides that the way to get what he wants is to systematically murder all of the public officials who are presently above him and in his path. This happens to be an idea that goes back at least to Shakespeare's *Macbeth*, and therefore I cannot protect that idea; I cannot foreclose all members of the public from developing something similar, and I shouldn't be allowed to. If you independently come up with a similar idea, how in the world are you going to know that your idea has been thought of by someone else and therefore you cannot develop it? The tangible expression of that idea, however, is protectable under the present system.

The expression of an idea is protectable, but the expression must be more than simply oral, or else it is not tangible and therefore not protectable. That is why you cannot go around bragging about the unique aspects of your brainstorm; it will not be unique for long, and if it is truly as fraught with possibilities as you imagine, someone to whom you have told the story, or someone who heard it from someone, will also recognize all of the virtues you have ascribed to it and develop it themselves. So let's protect your idea by having you reduce it to a writing and then filing for copyright protection for the writing. That is a very good idea, but how much of a writing does it have to be? Obviously, the briefer the writing, the greater the risk that someone will be able to copy it and make enough changes to convince a court and a jury that there has been no copying. If your writing is simply a statement that a politician murders his superiors in order to advance himself, then a copier can throw in a couple of changes, such as a murder of an inferior as well as of superiors, or claim public domain for the idea, and get away with it. The more detailed the writing, the more variations a copier will have to make in order to distinguish his work from yours, and the farther away from your idea will be the copy, which should suit you just fine. Remember, you are not looking for a lawsuit here, but rather protection from having your idea ripped off.

You have now been convinced that the best way to protect your idea is to reduce it to a written work, let's say a treatment if you plan to do a movie (a treatment is a brief synopsis, with some explanation of character and action, of the story the author proposes to later develop into a full fledged screenplay, complete with dialogue and scene descriptions), and then file an application with the Library of Congress for copy-right protection for that treatment. So far, so good.

Now you are ready for your next step, perhaps selling your treatment to a producer who will take it from there, and make the movie, paying you some amount for your troubles to date. This saves you from the terrible task of trying to raise money yourself, if you want to save yourself from that task. If you think you can raise enough money among your own friends, then you might be able to keep a larger share of the eventual profits for yourself. But what's this about not being able to just go to them and get the money? The law says that where anyone is soliciting funds, he or she must go through some incredibly complicated machinations that are almost impossible without an attorney. Worse, the attorney must follow so many regulations and draft disclosures in such complicated ways that the fees are very high indeed. What you need is what those in the money-raising business call "seed money,"—money to take the minimal first steps necessary to make the big effort to raise the big money necessary to finance the production of a movie. We are assuming now that you have not been able to interest a big movie producer in your project.

If you decide you are going to take the role of producer, you should know that you are buying many more headaches than the rather formidable task of raising money. You will have to make many creative as well as business decisions—hiring various support people, drawing up schedules, giving assurances to nervous investors—and in general will be driven crazy. However, let us stay with the money-raising problem for the moment. The large Hollywood studios, you may know, do not normally have to worry about raising money for a movie; rather, they sometimes have to worry about *spending* it. What I mean is that they have enough of that credibility we discussed before to have lines of credit at major banks, insurance companies and other lenders. Major studios, then, do not usually look for small investors who might want to buy one of 500 shares in a movie venture that needs five million dollars to complete. Independent producers do look for those kind of investors, but they often work from lists of investors that have been furnished to them by other producers. Believe it or not, there are national lists of regular investors in movie projects, which is not to say that the people on these lists will invest in anything that comes along; rather, they are somewhat discriminating. The point, however, is that it is normally difficult to find people who have money they are willing to invest in anything. It is more difficult to find people willing to invest in something as chancy as film (as distinguished from, say, real estate), and then even more difficult to persuade that group that of the film ventures they could sink money into, yours is the one that promises the greatest return.

Incidentally, what I meant before about major studios worrying about spending money is simply that they have stockholders, so that budgeting fifteen million dollars for a movie means having to explain to the stockholder owners why that budget has been unreasonably exceeded, if in fact it is exceeded.

Raising seed money is probably the worst obstacle any fledgling producer must hurdle. One of the problems is that most people are either reluctant to put up their own money, or they have been told by friends or other well-meaning acquaintances that the "big boys" don't play that way—they don't put up their own money, they spend only someone else's money, they are never personally "at risk." That is true, but again, the reason is that they don't have to put up their own money; they have enough credibility to raise money without difficulty and they have the resources to come up with the seed money to raise the main money. If you have enough confidence in your project to attempt to convince others to invest, you ought to be able to also sacrifice some of your own money. Seed money is important to put together an attractive package, to pay initial promotional and legal expenses, and to pay for the costs of attempting to raise the main fund that will finance the project.

In all of this, your experienced lawyer will render assistance. But since this is not meant to be a dissertation on how to make a movie, let us leave this subject to more thorough articles and books devoted to little else. Let us return, then, to what you should have some awareness of as far as general legal principles are concerned.

The discussion so far has dwelt on movies, but the general ideas are equally applicable to television scripts. In both movies and television, the artistic or creative end of the production deals mainly with the creation of scripts and the directing, or movement of actors and interpretation of the script's characters as dictated by the director. There are other creative aspects, such as costume and set design, but for purposes of this discussion we will limit ourselves to dealing with authors, directors and to a minor extent composers who may contribute a musical score to a film or television show. The rest of the behind-the-scenes people are involved in mechanical tasks for the most part, such as the building of sets, the moving of scenery, or the holding of microphones.

Directors of movies perform a different function from directors in television, but for both, there is normally no way they can protect what they have individually contributed to the final product. The point is that an author can retain some ownership in a script, and a composer can retain some interest in a musical composition, but what a director contributes is an intangible part of a whole, and it is the whole that will eventually be copyrighted as a movie. Since directors are also simply employees, in at least one sense, we need not dwell on them in a discussion of copyright ownership. The same general principle applies to costume designers who create in the context of the story, and while it may seem that they are able to separate out of any movie the costumes they have contributed, it doesn't work that way.

However, as noted, authors and composers have an unusual standing. They can do *other things* with their contributions to a film or a television show, without affecting the show in the least and perhaps even enhancing the commercial appeal of the main product. For example, Erich Segal was able to convert his screenplay for the movie *Love Story* into a book *after* the movie was completed and when it was about to be released. These other commercial possibilities are called "subsidiary rights," and the law allows you to deal with them or not deal with them, as you wish, but if you don't deal with them, you may be passing up untold opportunities to make money, achieve recognition, further the arts and perhaps make things easier for yourself the next time.

Subsididary rights are always negotiated when the two parties doing the negotiation are experienced, but they are often overlooked by the inexperienced, the naive, the careless. There are times when the subsidiary rights may prove to be even more valuable than the original work. We spoke at length about the situation where you are doing your own producing, and in that instance, you obviously have kept control of your own creation. Where you are relinquishing control to someone else, however, be it producer or agent, you should know what you are giving up and what you are keeping. The various lively arts are quite properly and beneficially parasitic, in that they feed off of themselves; movies are made from plays, plays from movies, movies become television series, television series become major motion pictures, books are made from all of these and music is recorded, used on soundtracks, played in the pit on Broaway, and made into theme songs and commercials. Who knows how long the current fad will continue of making wearing apparel featuring movie or television titles, themes or personalities. All of these uses can be permitted under controlled licenses from the creator of the underlying work that gave birth to all these commercial ventures, but only where the underlying rights have not been advertently or, more often, inadvertently given away or sold for a song. Given your sparkling idea for a movie or television show, it is possible that you also have a bonanza in commercial possibilities on your hands, and you can bet your beret that unless you take the proper steps to protect your property, the seasoned people with whom you deal will not hand them to you on a silver platter.

What do we mean by a license? Simply put, a license is a permission given by the owner of something to someone else for some limited use. It is distinguishable from a sale, which usually carries with it all the rights to the property, so the buyer no longer needs any permission from someone to do something with the property. A license is for a *limited* use, because unlimited use would again be too close to a sale. A license is often paid for by entering into a royalty arrangement. The person granting the license—the licensor—shares in profits or in all sales, and the person who is putting up the money or the facilities or in some other way incurring risks may part with some initial amount to buy the right to enter into the license over the desires of others who also want that right. This party, then, only pays if sales are made.

A discussion of licenses is very appropriate here because the right to grant those licenses is another of those subsidiary rights that you, the creator, don't want to lose. One of the best examples of the value of subsidiary rights is the sound track for the movie *Saturday Night Fever*, a low budget film that wasn't expected to do very well at the box office, with a music track by a singing and instrumental group that had been around for just about twenty years. The sound track album has sold over fifteen million copies, making the composers of most of the music, the Bee Gees, millions of dollars in royalties both as composers and as performers. The album also helped to make a record label, RSO. The benefits from a successful venture sometimes involve more than just money.

The point to be made here is that if you are the creator of what we referred to at the beginning of this article as a "fantastic idea", developing it yourself is going to require that you carefully educate yourself in the many aspects of the business. You've got too much to lose, potentially, if you don't.

You may, depending on the success of the project, make a good deal of money, or you may see nothing at all. If you are going to turn the work over to someone experienced, someone in whom you have confidence, that experience, and their work are going to cost you a chunk of your pie. Normally, authors get their scripts bought outright, which means that if you are a Nelson Algren, to cite an example, you can be offered a small chunk of money for the screen rights to a best-selling novel, *The Man With the Golden Arm*, then watch the movie do very, very well and realize that you have been paid a relative pittance. I should point out at this juncture that I have used the word "normally" very frequently in this article, but the word should not be taken to mean "invariably." Deals can be negotiated, and perhaps the worst mistake any author can make is to fall for the line, "But that's the way it's always done, and therefore we can't do it differently." You can bet your best typewriter that this line would not be used on Neil Simon. Among the many reasons to seek out someone with experience to help you is that inexperienced people simply cannot be sure that when they think they have been backed into a corner in negotiations, they really are back in that corner. If you are trying to sell your script, and some studio exec says, "Look, either take my offer or leave it—you get a flat fee or you get nothing," you don't want to use a ploy of holding out for a percentage of profits and have the exec say "Goodbye." If the script does not have, in the eyes of that exec, the great commercial possibilities you saw in it, you can very well kill your own deal, and therefore the entire future of your brainchild, by overnegotiation. Conversely, you don't want to say "I'll take it," only to learn later that you've given away the proverbial company store.

Assuming that you have found someone to negotiate with, you should find yourself someone with the right combination of experience and sympatico to help you negotiate a deal. The best way to sell a literary property, whether play, screenplay or what have you, is through a literary agent, unless you personally have extraordinary contacts in the business. Agents know their markets, usually, and have much more credibility than submissions that come in "over the transom," that is, unsolicited and sent by unknowns. This means, among other things, that the submission is more likely to be read if it comes from an agent. Unfortunately agents don't simply "take on" anyone who asks, so getting an agent isn't all that easy. If you find one who agrees to handle you, he or she might also be able to negotiate your deal, including subsidiary rights, for you, or you can have your lawyer do it. If you are at a loss as to where to turn initially, there are some excellent sources of information such as a magazine entitled *Writer's Guide*, that will tell you where various markets are, the nature of the items bought by those markets, and other invaluable aids.

During the course of the negotiations, you will learn about all sorts of uses of material, such as first serial rights, foreign language rights, the possibility of developing the script in the form of a sequel or what is being called a "prequel"—a story using the same characters as the first story, but picking up the action *before* the first story's beginning. Through all of the dickering, you might get the idea that if everyone is making this much of a fuss over a script, it really must be worth a lot. Not necessarily true. Purchasers normally try to negotiate as much as possible before any purchase commitments are made, even where the material being purchased is judged relatively worthless, because if these small details are ignored, you can bet it will be *that* deal that turns into an unexpected, incredible success, after which the producer is in no position to negotiate a fair deal.

It is obviously to the advantage of the writer to keep as many rights as he or she can in any negotiation, because if for any reason the one right sold, for example, the screen rights, hits it big, all the other rights become very valuable and can be negotiated separately and with other companies and other media. Writers often have more leverage to negotiate than they think they have. It is an often-heard fear that writers do not want to get an attorney involved in negotiations because they don't want the deal to become so complicated that the would-be purchaser becomes totally turned off and decides not to buy. This fear is groundless with reputable buyers, because dealings with established writers always include dealings with attorneys or agents, or both, and it is expected. The fly-by-night operators will object, but no dealings should be had with them, anyway. It is occasionally true that an over-zealous or inexperienced attorney will kill a deal because of insistence on holding on to an unreasonable position, but even in that situation the writer can exercise some control by occasionally reminding the lawyer who is paying the bill for the lawyer's services.

Where there has been a sale of movie or television rights to a literary property, control over the development of the property from then until the final product is ready for market is usually lost. This is because the particular purchaser wants the freedom to make a movie or show based on his or her own vision of the final package. This control could have a dramatic effect on the earnings potential of the property, but it can't be helped under normal circumstances, and there is a real risk that an author can watch a concept that was lovingly and slowly nurtured from conception to final writing, die or be corrupted in the hands of a total stranger. It is at times like those that an author can only hope that he or she is not a "one book" writer.

What we have discussed in this article is, in very general terms, the conception of an idea, the reduction of that idea to a tangible form, and then the disposition of that form in some fashion, hopefully for fun and profit. Our discussion has focused on the legal pitfalls, but there are many other things to be wary of. To review, a creator should not disseminate an idea too widely, lest it be stolen by someone adept at altering the original work just enough to avoid liability for copyright infringement. The idea should be reduced to a tangible expression to make it eligible for copyright protection, and while we have uniformly been discussing that expression in terms of a writing, it need not necessarily be that. It could easily be a film, even if crude and homemade, or it could be a recording. In any event, the expression whatever its form, should then be registered with the U.S. Copyright Office, a part of the Library of Congress, and a copyright notice should be placed on the work itself, in a place reasonably calculated to give notice to anyone seeing the work that copyright protection is being claimed. I mentioned earlier the concept of mailing a copy of a work to oneself as a method of copyright protection, and perhaps it should be explained that this procedure is legally meaningless—the only good it does lies in helping to prove a date of creation of a work. To illustrate, let's suppose that I wrote a work in December, and now I believe that Mr. X has stolen my material. Mr. X's defense is that he wrote his without seeing mine and it was written in January, *following* my writing. As an aid in proving when I wrote my piece, I could hand an envelope to the judge, previously unopened, addressed to me and sent by me, registered mail, in which is a copy of my work. The judge would then be able to check the date on the envelope and probably agree with my contention that I did indeed write my piece in December. Other than as an aid in proving date of origin, the mailing procedure has no legal significance.

Now we have our work created, reduced to a tangible form of expression and copyrighted, with an appropriate copyright notice. The next step is to sell the work, assuming it is a screenplay or screen treatment, for further development, or alternatively attempt to develop it independently. If it is sold to a producer for further development, the trick is to retain as many subsidiary rights as the author possibly can, in the hope that these rights will be worth a great deal of money if the main property hits. If the decision is to attempt to develop the property independently, then any money-raising activities must follow the complex and cumbersome laws relating to those activities, under penalty of having to pay severely in money and in some cases even spend time in jail. Producing it independently, you will probably also have to give away innumerable pieces of the project in order to attract and keep really good people—artists and technicians—who are used to demanding and getting those pieces. This means that, as a practical matter, if you have offered fifty percent of your profit pie to would-be investors, as is usually done, then when a director, or a star, or a composer, says "I'll work for so many dollars *and* several points (percentage points)," you'll wind up giving away those points out of *your* share of the pie. If you do this often enough, as you might where you are looking for good support people, you may find yourself with very little left of a project for which you have knocked yourself out. Of course, you have also observed all of the formidable legal requirements imposed on money raisers, and have been forced to paint such a dismal picture of your venture in the prospectus sent to would-be investors that you are having second thoughts yourself. Then once the money is raised, it must be handled with such care that you may once again wonder if it's worth it.

Your only consolation might be that of the millions before you who have tried to do exactly what you are doing, some infinitesimal portion actually did make it, against overwhelming odds. If they could do it, you can, too. Maybe. But you will increase those odds against you if you have to finish your work from the inside of a jail cell, and so it makes good sense to get some expert help at the outset.

E. Leonard Rubin

Visual Arts & the Law

In the last decade art has become big business.[1] Many investors have turned to the collection of art objects as a hedge against inflation because the value of art has appreciated faster than that of more traditional investments.[2] Intensified business interest in the arts has highlighted the legal problems artists encounter in the production and distribution of their work. Gone are the days when the artist could dismiss as "crass," "commercial," or "irrelevant," the legal and business matters which are inevitable parties to the creative process.

This chapter will provide a broad overview of various legal matters that are important to the visual artist. Of course, this presentation is no substitute for seeking competent legal or other professional counsel as particular situations may dictate. On the other hand, the ability to identify legal problems may well prompt the artist to seek help when needed, and to appreciate the relationship between art and the law.[3]

Art Law and the Definition of Art

The emergence of "art law" has emphasized the interdependence of these two disciplines.[4] A steady flow of literature in the area has developed,[5] and with the passage of the Copyright Revision Act of 1976 (the "1976 Act")[6] many of the nagging problems of a legal "definition of art" have been resolved.[7] For our purposes the definition of the "visual arts" will echo the definition set forth in "Works of the Visual Arts" under the copyright regulations:

This class [new Class VA] includes all published and unpublished pictorial, graphic, and sculptural works. Examples: two dimensional and three dimensional works of the fine, graphic, and applied arts; photographs; prints and art reproductions; maps, globes, and charts; technical drawings, diagrams, and models; and pictorial or graphic labels and advertisements.[8]

COPYRIGHT LAW

The law of copyrights is the single most important area of visual arts law. The artist who is familiar with its provisions is in an excellent position to exercise and protect his or her rights. This section will recount the history of copyright law in the United States, and will describe and analyze the provisions most relevant to the visual artist.[9]

History of United States Copyright Law
Copyright law in the United States may be traced to the law passed by the English Parliament in 1710, known as the *Statute of Anne*.[10] Before federal legislation in the area, many of the states had adopted copyright laws patterned after this English statute. Federal uniformity was introduced by Article I, Section 8, Clauses 8 and 18 of the United States Constitution, which provides that:

The Congress shall have Power . . .
    To promote the Progress of Science and useful Arts, by securing for limited Times to Authors and Inventors the exclusive Right to their respective Writings and Discoveries;
    . . . —And To make all Laws which shall be necessary and proper for carrying into Execution the foregoing Powers, and all the Powers vested by this Constitution in the Government of the United States, or in any Department or Officer thereof.

The first federal copyright law was enacted in 1790. This law granted copyright protection to originally created maps, charts and books, giving authors and proprietors of such works the exclusive right of printing, publishing and vending for a period of 14 years, a term which could be renewed for a second 14 years. There were general revisions of United States copyright law in 1831, 1870 and 1909, and amendments to existing law in 1802, 1834, 1856, 1873, 1891 and 1897.

The Copyright Revision Act of 1976 was the first major revision of the copyright laws of the United States since the passage of the 1909 Act. A 1973 Report of the United States Senate Committee on the Judiciary noted that the 1909 Act was archaic because, "Many significant developments in technology and communication . . . [had] . . . rendered that law clearly inadequate to the needs of the country today."[11]

The arduous task of adapting the 1909 Act to 20th century technological realities began in 1955 when Congress appropriated funds "for a comprehensive program of research and studies by the Copyright Office as the groundwork for such revision".[12] Some 35 studies were produced over the following years,[13] and in 1967 the House passed its version of a copyright revision bill, followed in 1974 by a Senate bill which differed from the House version in a number of specific areas. A conference committee produced a single version and on October 19, 1976, the President signed into law Public Law 94-553 ("An Act for the general revision of the copyright law").

Copyright Revision Act of 1976

Definition of Copyright

A copyright is the exclusive right of ownership of works created by human intelligence.[14] The standards for copyrightability of a work are *originality* and *fixation* in a tangible form, terms purposely left loosely defined in the 1976 Act. A work is entitled to copyright protection if it represents some degree of creative authorship and has been reduced to a fixed form.[15] Copyrightability is a concept which takes form and meaning from society's changing perceptions of "originality" and "fixation in tangible form." Artwork considered not copyrightable today may qualify for such protection tomorrow.[16]

Under the 1976 Act, "[a] work is 'fixed' in a tangible medium of expression when its embodiment in a copy . . . , by or under the authority of the author, is sufficiently permanent or stable to permit it to be perceived, reproduced, or otherwise communicated for a period of more than transitory duration."[17] At the same time, "[a] work is 'created' when it is fixed in a copy . . . for the first time; where a work is prepared over a period of time, the portion of it that has been fixed at any particular time constitutes the work as of that time, and where the work has been prepared in different versions, each version constitutes a separate work."[18] Copyright protection, then, is accorded to artists' original works at the moment they are created.

Federal Preemption
The 1976 Act specifically provides that " . . . all legal or equitable rights that are equivalent to any of the exclusive rights within the general scope of copyright . ." are preempted by the new copyright law, and that " . . . no person is entitled to any such right or equivalent right in any such work under the common law or statutes of any State."[19] Until passage of the 1976 Act, a dual system of copyright protection for the works of authors had existed; common law or state copyright protection, which covered unpublished works of authors, and the federal copyright law which protected the copyrightable works of authors in their published state. Today, the 1976 Act embodies a uniform system for the copyright protection of the works of artists.[20]

Duration of Copyright Protection[21]
Under the 1909 Act's dual system of copyright protection, works registered in the unpublished form were accorded copyright protection for a maximum of 56 years from the date of registration (28 years plus a renewal term of 28 years).

Published works were given the same protection, except that the term was measured from the date the work was first published. For an author to receive maximum protection for his or her unpublished and published works under the old copyright law, an actual renewal registration had to be filed by the copyright owner.

Except for certain works,[22] the 1976 Act has not retained the renewal system of the old 1909 Act, and copyright protection for works created on or after January 1, 1978 begins at the moment of creation and extends for a non-renewable term ending 50 years after the author's death. "Joint works," or works by more than one author are entitled to copyright protection for 50 years after the death of the last surviving author; and anonymous, pseudonymous and works for hire are entitled to copyright protection for 100 years from the moment of creation or 75 years from the date of first publication, whichever event occurs first.[23] Works already in the "public domain" (works which lost their copyrightability because they, for example, were "published" without a copyright notice under the old 1909 Act) cannot be copyrighted under the 1976 Act. Under the 1976 Act, all copyright terms run to December 31 of the year in which they would otherwise expire.[24]

Works created but not published or copyrighted before January 1, 1978, and which have not entered the public domain are given the same protection as other works except that "In no case . . . shall the term of copyright in such a work expire before December 31, 2002 . . . "[25] If such works are published on or before December 31, 2002, " . . . the term of copyright shall not expire before December 31, 2027."[26]

Works copyrighted before January 1, 1978—the effective date of the 1976 Act—are accorded protection for a first term of 28 years from the date of copyright protection obtained by publication or registration, with a right to renew the copyright an additional 47 years, or a total of 75 years of copyright protection. Copyrights in their first 28 year term on January 1, 1978, will have to be specifically renewed at the end of the 28 year period to receive the additional 47 year renewal term; copyrights that were in their second 28 year term on January 1, 1978 are automatically extended to last a total of 75 years without the need for a specific renewal registration.[27] What should be remembered is that copyrights existing in their first term as of January 1, 1978 must be specifically renewed by December 31 of the year the copyright would otherwise expire in order for the copyright to be extended for another 47 years.[28]

Because the copyright duration rules are complex, artists should consult with their attorneys to determine the copyright status of all works created and/or copyrighted before or after January 1, 1978, in order to prepare a schedule showing which copyrights require renewal, and when each copyright will expire.

Subject Matter of Copyright
Under the 1976 Act, copyright protection applies to original works of authorship fixed in any tangible form now known or later developed, among them, pictorial, graphic, and sculptural works, and motion pictures and other audiovisual works.[29] "Original work of authorship" entitled to copyright protection does not " . . .extend to any idea, procedure, process, system, method of operation, concept, principle or discovery . . . "[30] In other words, mere ideas are uncopyrightable.

Joint and Derivative Works and Collections
A "joint work" is defined as " . . . a work prepared by two or more authors with the intention that their contributions be merged into inseparable or interdependent parts of a unitary whole."[31] As noted earlier, the copyright to work created on or after January 1, 1978, by joint authors lasts 50 years after the death of the last surviving author. Unlike copyrights in collections (which are discussed below) the rights of joint authors are merged, and each author may exercise the rights of copyright ownership subject only to an accounting to the other joint owners.[32]

A "derivative work" is " . . . a work based upon one or more preexisting works, such as [an] . . . art reproduction . . . or any other form in which a work may be recast, transformed, or adapted."[33] As will be discussed later, the owner of a copyright has the exclusive right to make a work derived from a particular copyrighted work, but that copyright owner may also authorize others to prepare a derivative work without necessarily losing any of the other rights he or she is entitled to under the 1976 Act.

A "collective work" is defined as " . . . a work, such as a periodical issue, anthology, or encyclopedia, in which a number of contributions, constituting separate and independent works in themselves, are assembled into a collective whole."[34] The owner of the copyright in a collective work (for example, the editor or publishing company) acquires only the privilege of reproducing and distributing the contribution in the collective work in question, a revision of such work, or a later collective work in the same series. Certain 'residual' rights remain with the individual contributor, even in the absence of a separate copyright notice on the individual contribution.[35]

National Origin
Published works are entitled to copyright protection under the 1976 Act if on the date of first publication, one of the authors is a United States citizen or a resident of the United States, or is a citizen or resident of a foreign nation that is a party to a copyright treaty to which the United States is also a party.[36] Works of authors in the unpublished state are accorded United States copyright protection without regard to the nationality or domicile of the author.[37] American artists living abroad automatically have United States copyright protection at the moment of artistic creation.

Ownership in General
The bundle of rights enumerated in the 1976 Act remain initially with the author or authors of a work[38] until there is a transfer of the specific right or rights in question.[39] Copyright ownership may be transferred in whole or in part by any means of conveyance, including conveyance by license, assignment, mortgage, or by any other means (as by will or

by the laws of intestate succession when the copyright owner dies without a will).[40] The 1976 Act also specifically recognizes the divisibility of copyrights; that is, any of the exclusive rights of copyright ownership may be subdivided and transferred separately, entitling the owner of a particular exclusive right to all pertinent protections and remedies accorded to the original copyright owner.[41] With proper planning, the divisibility of copyrights may present the artist with the opportunity to maximize his or her economic return from each individual copyright. The artist should find a competent attorney when attempting to capitalize on his or her copyright bundle, because transfers of copyright ownership must be evidenced in writing and recorded in the Copyright Office.

Until enactment of the 1976 Act, the concept of "for-hire works" created trouble for artists. Who owns the copyright when the artist has been commissioned or otherwise engaged to produce an art product? The 1976 Act gives copyright ownership to the "employer" of the artist in such situations *unless* the parties have agreed otherwise in a signed, written instrument.[42] If, in fact, a commissioned artist is to retain some or all of the bundle of exclusive copyrights under the 1976 Act, that understanding with the commissioning "employer" must be written and signed by both parties. If employer and artist fail to reach an understanding about who owns the various exclusive copyrights, the employer, *not* the artist, will become "author" and owner of *all* of the exclusive rights provided under the 1976 Act. Once again, careful business and legal counsel can prevent such problems.

Transfers of Copyright Ownership
As noted before, a "transfer of copyright ownership" is defined as " . . .an assignment, mortgage, exclusive license [but not a nonexclusive license], or any other conveyance, alienation, or hypothecation of a copyright or of any of the exclusive rights comprised in a copyright, whether or not it is limited in time or place of effect . . . "[43] Such transfer must be

written,[44] and though not required, should be notarized.[45] If the document bears the actual signature of the person signing, or if it is accompanied by a sworn or official certification that it is a true copy of the original signed instrument it may be recorded in the Copyright Office.[46] The recording of transfers in the Copyright Office establishes a conclusion of law which precludes contradiction (called "constructive notice") of the facts stated in the document.[47] Recording also is a prerequisite to the institution of an infringement suit brought by the person claiming copyright ownership by virtue of the transfer.[48]

Termination of Transfers and Licenses
Unlike the old 1909 Act, the 1976 Act does not have a copyright term renewal system. Under the 1909 Act, an author who had transferred his rights during the first 28 year term of his or her copyright would receive back all of those rights at the end of 28 years. He or she would then be in position either to renegotiate an agreement for use of the copyright in the second 28 year term, or simply to take back the copyright and renew it for him or her self. The 1976 Act simply gives an author the right to terminate a transfer or license within a specified time so long as he or she gives advance notice of his or her intention to make such an election.[49] Generally, a grant may be terminated at any time during a 5 year period beginning at the end of 35 years from the date of execution of the grant,[50] as long as notice under rules of the Register of Copyrights is served not less than 2 or more than 10 years before the termination date of the grant.[51] The 1976 Act also provides for termination of grants of copyrights in their first or renewal term as of January 1, 1978, the effective date of the Act.[52] Complex rules determine who may terminate a grant, and how the task should be timed and documented.

Exclusive Rights of Copyright Owners
The owner of a copyright has a bundle of exclusive rights under the 1976 Act. They include:

(1) the right to reproduce the copyrighted work in "copies";

(2) the right to prepare derivative works based on the copyrighted work;

(3) the right to "distribute" copies of the copyrighted work to the public by sale or other transfer of ownership, or by rental, lease, or lending;

(4) in the case of pictorial, graphic, or sculptural works, including the individual images of a motion picture or other audiovisual work, the right to "display" the copyrighted work publicly.[53]

The exclusive rights may be exercised by the copyright owner personally, and he or she alone may authorize others to exercise those rights.

The 1976 Act defines "copies" as " . . . material objects . . . in which a work is fixed by any method now known or later developed, and from which the work can be perceived, reproduced, or otherwise communicated, either directly or with the aid of a machine or device," and " . . . includes the material object . . . in which the work is first fixed."[54] "Publication" for the purposes of the 1976 Act means " . . . the distribution of copies . . . of a work to the public by sale or other transfer of ownership, or by rental, lease, or lending" and includes "[t]he offering to distribute copies . . . to a group of persons for purposes of further distribution, public performance, or public display," though "[a] public performance or display of a work does not of itself constitute publication."[55] To "display a work publicly" is defined in part as " . . . to display it at a place open to the public or at any place where a substantial number of persons outside of a normal circle of a family and its social acquaintance is gathered."[56]

Limitations on this bundle of exclusive rights include the "fair use" doctrine (use of copyrighted works for purposes such as criticism, comment, news reporting, teaching (including multiple copies for classroom use, scholarship, or research),[57] and the reproduction of copies by libraries and archives.[58]

The Visual Arts Under the 1976 Act

"Pictorial, Graphic, and Sculptural Works"
Under the 1976 Act, copyrightable works under the category of "pictorial, graphic, and sculptural works" include:

... two-dimensional and three-dimensional works of fine, graphic, and applied art, photographs, prints and art repro-ductions, maps, globes, charts, technical drawings, diagrams, and models. Such works shall include works of artistic crafts-manship insofar as their form but not their mechanical or utilitarian aspects are concerned; the design of a useful article, as defined in this section, shall be considered a pic-torial, graphic, or sculptural work only if, and only to the extent that, such design incorporates pictorial, graphic, and sculptural features that can be identified separately from, and are capable of existing independently of, the utilitarian aspects of the article.[59]

Pictorial, graphic and sculptural works are specifically listed as a category of "works of authorship" to which copyright protection applies.[60] They are designated as "Class VA: Works of the Visual Arts" under the new classification system for copyright registrations effective January 1, 1978[61]. Included in the "pictorial, graphic and sculptural works" category are etchings, woodcuts, silkscreens and other art reproduction techniques, provided that the work of art or craftsmanship itself is original and copyrightable. Photo-graphs are likewise copyrightable under this category. In all categories copyrightability does not hinge on the artistic quality of the work, but rather on whether it is an original work in a tangible medium of expression.[62] As discussed before, copyright protection under the 1976 Act exists at the moment of artistic creation; that is, the artist receives copy-right protection the moment his work is fixed in any tangible form.

Scope of Exclusive Rights
The 1976 Act gives the copyright owner of a pictorial, graphic, or sculptural work the exclusive right to reproduce

the work in copies, including the right to reproduce it in or on any kind of article, useful or not.[63] Reproduction of art works is the exclusive right of the copyright owner and includes the making of a print, lithograph, or etching from a copyrighted painting, photograph or sculpture. Once again, only the copyright owner may reproduce or authorize the reproduction of his copyrighted pictorial, graphic, and sculptural work, and until such work has entered the public domain, no reproductions or copies may be made from it.[64]

Works of Art in Useful Articles
In 1954, the United States Supreme Court in considering works of art in "useful articles," held that only the *art* and not the material article or object itself could be copyrighted.[65] Defining a "useful article" in part as " . . . an article having an intrinsic utilitarian function that is not merely to portray the appearance of the article or to convey information,"[66] the 1976 Act adopts the Supreme Court's position that only the *art* in a useful article (e.g., the art work fixed in a painted doorknob which is part of the sculptural installation) and *not the article itself* (the doorknob or any piece of useful article in the installation) may be copyrighted[67]. Recently, though, Congressional legislation has been introduced which would extend copyright protection to ornamental designs embodied in useful articles.[68]

Copyright Owner and Ownership of Material Object
Unlike prior law,[69] ownership of a copyright under the 1976 Act is distinct from ownership of the material object in which the work is embodied or fixed.[70] Consequently, transfer of ownership of the material object, including the copy in which the work is first fixed, does not convey any of the exclusive copyrights.[71] Likewise, in the absence of an agreement, transfer of ownership of a copyright or any of the exclusive rights under a copyright does not convey property rights to any material object. This changes the old law which held that transfer of the material object (e.g., the oil painting) to a purchaser automatically meant transfer of the underlying copyright. The 1976 Act presumes that the artist

has reserved all exclusive copyrights unless such rights have been transferred, evidenced by a written instrument. Though the owner of the material object of a copyright (say, an oil painting) may sell or otherwise dispose of the material object at his own discretion,[72] and while he has limited rights of "display,"[73] he may not "reproduce," publish, or exercise any of the exclusive rights which belong to the copyright owner (the artist).

Mechanics of Copyright Protection

Copyright Notice

Under the old 1909 Act, the required copyright notice had to be affixed to each copy published or offered for sale, and if the copyright notice was omitted or incorrectly placed, the claim of copyright was automatically lost. The 1976 Act departs from the rigid requirements of prior law, simply requiring a notice of copyright on publicly distributed copies of a work.[74] As discussed below, omission of the copyright notice and other technical mistakes which under prior law would have proven fatal,[75] no longer will defeat the copyright claim.

Form of Notice

Under the 1976 Act, for visually perceptible copies of a work, the copyright notice consists of three elements:

(1) the symbol © (the letter C in a circle), or the word "Copyright", or the abbreviation "Copr."; and

(2) the year of first publication, which means[76] the year in which there is a first distribution of copies of a work to the public by sale or other transfer of ownership, or by rental, lease, or lending, or by offering to distribute copies to a group of persons for purposes of further distribution or public display; and

(3) the name of the owner of the copyright in the work, or an abbreviation by which the name can be recognized, or a generally known alternative designation of the owner.[77]

Position of Copyright Notice
The 1976 Act gives the Register of Copyrights discretion to promulgate rules and regulations regarding positions of the copyright notice on various types of works.[78] For years disgruntled by the defacement of their works by placement of copyright notices, most artists simply ignored the copyright notice requirements. Under "proposed" regulations issued by the Copyright Office on December 15, 1977, and published shortly thereafter,[79] for pictorial, graphic and sculptural works, it is an acceptable method of affixation and positioning of the copyright notice if:

(1) the work is reproduced in two-dimensional copies, and the notice is affixed directly or by means of a label cemented, sewn, or otherwise permanently secured to the front *or back* of the copies, or to any backing, mounting, matting, framing, or other material to which the copies are permanently attached or in which they are permanently housed;

(2) the work is reproduced in three-dimensional copies, and the notice is affixed directly or by means of a label cemented, sewn, or otherwise permanently secured to any visible portion of the work, or to any base, mounting, framing, or other material on which the copies are permanently attached or in which they are permanently housed;

(3) the work, because of size or the physical characteristics of the materials used, makes it impossible or extremely impracticable to affix a notice to the copies directly or by means of permanent label, the notice may appear on a tag of durable material attached to the copy with sufficient permanency that it will remain with the copy during the entire time it passes through its normal channels of commerce;

(4) the work is reproduced in copies consisting of sheet-like or strip material bearing multiple or continuous reproductions, and the notice is applied (i) to the reproduction itself, (ii) to the margin, selvage, or reverse side of the material at frequent and regular intervals, or (iii) if the

material contains neither a selvage nor a reverse side, to tags or labels attached to the copies and to any spools, reels, or containers housing them in such a way that a notice is visible during the entire time the copies pass through their normal channels of commerce.

(5) if the work is permanently housed in a container, such as a game or puzzle box, a notice reproduced on the permanent container is acceptable.

The basic rule to follow in positioning the copyright notice to a work of fine or visual arts is to place it in such a way that a reasonable person of ordinary intelligence would discover it during a reasonable examination of the work. Under the proposed rules, then, a copyright notice permanently legible on the reverse side of a canvas would secure copyright protection to the author of an oil painting.

Copyright Notice Omissions and Mistakes
Omission of the copyright notice[80] and errors in name or date in copyrights[81] no longer automatically defeat a claim of copyright. Omission of the copyright notice does not defeat the copyright if " . . . no more than a relatively small number of copies . . . " have been distributed to the public, or if registration for the work is made within 5 years after publication and a reasonable effort has been made to add the notice to the copies publicly distributed. If no effort has been made to place the copyright notice on copies of works which have been publicly distributed, then the work enters the public domain and the claim of copyright is defeated. In other words, if an artist forgets to put the copyright notice on his or her publicly distributed works, he or she has 5 years to make a reasonable effort to place the copyright notice on those works, or the claim of copyright will be defeated. Omission of the copyright notice, even if corrected within the 5 year grace period, will limit the amount of damages recoverable from a so-called "innocent infringer." [82]

Use of the wrong name in a copyright notice affects neither the validity nor the ownership of the copyright, but innocent infringers have a complete defense if they are in fact misled in dealing with the person named on the notice. An antedated, incorrect date in a copyright would mean that any statutory term measured from the year of first publication would be computed from the year given in the notice. In the case of postdated, incorrect dates where the year in the copyright notice is more than one year later than the year of first publication, the notice is treated as if it had been completely omitted.

Registration and Deposit of Copyrights
While the old 1909 Act combined deposit and registration into a single requirement, the 1976 Act establishes a mandatory deposit requirement for works published with a copyright notice, and makes registration for both published and unpublished works voluntary rather than mandatory.[83] There are penalties for failing to make requisite deposits of publicly distributed works which carry a copyright notice, and certain disadvantages are attached to late registration of copyright. But unlike the 1909 Act, the copyright claim exists at the moment of creation without any further affirmative act on the part of the "author."

Registration of a claim of copyright in a work may be made at any time during the life of the copyright by filing an application, and by making the required deposit of copies accompanied by the requisite fee. In general, an action for infringement of a copyright may not be maintained unless the copyright has been registered, and innocent infringers are protected when copyrights have not been registered or have not been filed on time.

The 1976 Act imposes fines of up to $2,500 for public distribution of copies of works carrying a copyright notice when the required copies of the work have not been deposited with the Library of Congress within 3 months of publication in the United States. Penalties under the 1976 Act are assessed only after a written demand for the required deposits has been made by the Register of Copyrights.[84]

Substantial relief has been accorded visual artists with

respect to deposit requirements. For registration deposits of published and unpublished works, the Register of Copyrights will accept identifying material instead of "copies" of the work. "Identifying material" means photographic prints, transparencies, photostats, drawings, or similar two-dimensional reproductions or renderings of a work, in a form visually perceivable without the aid of a machine or device. In the case of pictorial or graphic works, identifying material must reproduce the actual colors employed in the work; for other works, black and white identifying material will suffice. Identifying material must meet certain size, title and dimension requirements, and the identifying material must show the location of the copyright notice on the work.[85] In the case of published pictorial or graphic works, for example, the requirement is satisfied if one copy *or* identifying material is deposited, if the individual author is the owner of the copyright, and either less than five copies of the work have been published or the work has been published and sold or offeed for sale in a limited edition consisting of no more than 300 numbered copies.[86] The deposit requirement for limited edition and three-dimensional works (e.g., sculpture and work in useful articles) may be satisfied by depositing satisfactory identifying material,[87] and there is an administrative procedure available for requesting exemptions from the deposit requirement.[88]

Application Forms
Application forms under the 1976 Act may be obtained by writing or calling the Copyright Office, Library of Congress, Washington, D.C. 20559. (Also available from the Copyright Office are informative "circulars" explaining each facet of the law and procedures of copyright.) These forms should be filled out carefully. Proper postage should be provided for mailings to the Copyright Office since the provision which in essence assured free postage was repealed effective January 1, 1978.[89]

Infringement
The infringement and remedies sections of the 1976 Act[90]

give the legal or beneficial owner of a copyright the right to enforce judicially his bundle of exclusive rights against those who violate ("infringe") those rights. Depending on the nature of the facts in each case, the copyright owner is entitled to receive damages and recovery of profits from the infringer. Other possible remedies include impounding and destruction of infringing articles (i.e., destruction of un-authorized "copies"); injunctions to prevent future acts of infringement; and imposition by the court of stiff criminal penalties and prison terms for persons who infringe a copy-right willfully and for purposes of commercial advantage or private financial gain.[91]

Copyright Law in a Nutshell
Here is a summary of the portions of copyright law that are relevant to the visual artist:

(1) The copyright laws in the United States have historical roots in the 1710 English *Statute of Anne,* and stem from Article I, Section 8, Clauses 8 and 18 of the United States Constitution.

(2) A "copyright" is the right given by law for the author of a work, for a limited period of time, to exercise dominion and control over the fruits of his intelligence. It is an intangible, incorporeal right and exclusive privilege to publish and copy an artistic 'concept' fixed in a material object.

(3) The 1976 Act preempts state and common law copyright protections, creating a single national system for all copy-rightable work to be protected from the date of creation and during each stage of creation as the artistic concept becomes visually perceivable in a fixed form.

(4) The visual arts are specifically a subject of copyright protection under the rubric of "pictorial, graphic, and sculp-tural works."

(5) For works "created" after the effective date of the 1976 Act (i.e., January 1, 1978), the copyright endures for the life of the author plus 50 years. For "joint works" the copyright

term endures for the life of the last surviving author plus 50 years. Anonymous, pseudonymous, and made-for-hire works have a copyright term of 75 years from first publication or 100 years from creation, whichever is shorter. For preexisting copyrights a renewal term of 47 years is available if the work was in its first 28 year term on January 1, 1978. For works in their second 28 year term on January 1, 1978, the term automatically extends to make the original copyright last for a total term of 75 years.

(6) Ownership and transfer documents relating to copyrights may be recorded in the Copyright Office. Copyrights may be transferred with limitations in time or place of effect, since there is now statutory recognition of the divisibility of copyright. For example, the owner of a copyright first fixed in an oil painting may transfer the exclusive right to make copies of the work in lithographs in a particular city for a specified period of time.

(7) Copyright transfers and licenses granted by authors may be terminated by the author during a 5 year period beginning at the end of 35 years from the date of the grant or date of publication, whichever is applicable under the circumstances. There are notice and recording requirements for such terminations.

(8) Notice, deposit and registration requirements differ from earlier copyright law. Mistakes and omissions in the copyright notice do not necessarily destroy the claim of copyright, and generally the copyright owner has five years to make a reasonable effort to correct any such mistakes or omissions. Registration and deposit are separate formalities which may be combined in one effort, and the Copyright Office has granted substantial relief to visual artists to deposit "identifying material" instead of actual "copies" of copyrighted works.

(9) The copyright owner is given several statutory remedies to prevent others from infringing the copyright and for col-

lecting damages from those who do violate this bundle of exclusive rights.

CONTRACT LAW FOR THE VISUAL ARTIST

Basic Contract Law Principles

There are many popular conceptions about contracts. Many people believe, for example, that an invoice or similar commercial document is "only" a receipt, and the "fine print" on the reverse side of such a "piece of paper" is a "mere formality." Such popular conceptions quickly change to rude awakenings when the "fine print" on a "piece of paper" becomes the basis for a lawsuit by someone enforcing the terms and conditions of the "contract" on the reverse side.

A contract may be defined as " . . . a promise or a set of promises for the breach of which the law gives a remedy, or the performance of which the law in some way recognizes as a duty."[92] Simply stated, a contract is a legally enforceable promise, while a promise to be legally enforceable must be a contract.

While a contract may be either written or oral, an oral contract may not be enforceable if its subject matter is of a nature legally requiring a writing of some sort.[93] A contract must have the *mutual assent* of two or more persons competent to contract to perform some *legal act* which is *mutually obligatory* on the parties.

Of the many types of contracts, consignment contracts are of particular interest to the visual artist because they are the type of relationship often formed between artists and art galleries.[94] In a consignment contract, one person (the "consignor", such as an artist) sends property to another person (the "consignee," such as an art gallery). The person receiving the property (consignee) then holds the property on behalf of the owner (consignor) subject to disposition of the property as the owner/consignor may instruct. The ownership ("title") of the consignor's property in the hands of the consignee remains with the consignor.

The purpose of a good contract is to anticipate and solve the problems which the contracting parties may encounter, in an effort to avoid later courtroom battles. The very process of contract negotiation helps to identify those problems, and establishes bases of agreement to resolve future disputes. Contract formation thus has both a prophylactic and therapeutic purpose.

Tradition, unequal bargaining power, and ignorance of the law have kept many artists from entering into written agreements with galleries. Unfortunately, the acquisition and disposition of artistic property has largely gone undocumented, creating undue confusion and (sometimes) ill will. Knowledge of contract law and contract provisions gives the artist a powerful advantage in dealings with galleries. At the very least, problems may be spotted by the artist as they arise, so that legal counsel may be sought.

Artist/Gallery Contractual Relations

Much has been written about artist/gallery contractual relations,[95] and several "standard form contracts"[96] have been devised. The need to formalize artist-gallery relations has become increasingly apparent since passage of the 1976 Act, with its statutory recognition of copyright divisibility and its new recording requirements Not only must visual art work shown in galleries receive full copyright protection; that protection should also maximize commercial gains for *both* artist and gallery/dealer. Recent court cases, including the litigation involving the estate of artist Mark Rothko,[97] have dramatized the problems faced by artists and their heirs when they enter into relationships with galleries or dealers. Contractual relations based on formal, negotiated agreements rather than on tradition and trade usage will help to alleviate such problems.

Artist/Gallery Consignment Agreements

The following issues should be considered by the artist and

his or her lawyer when negotiating and drafting a consignment agreement:

(1) Section 2-326 of the Uniform Commercial Code should be
carefully examined and appropriate language incorporated
into the contract so that consigned art pieces in the hands of
the gallery do not become subject to the claims of the
gallery's creditors. Some states, New York for example,
exempt the artist/dealer-consignor/consignee relationship
from the operation of Section 2-326 (Section 219-a of New
York's General Business Law). In other states it may be necessary to state in the contract that the gallery will establish a
procedure clearly and publicly distinguishing items that are
on consignment from an artist, from items that belong to the
gallery. The artist should also ask his attorney to determine
whether filing of "financing statements" for gallery-
consigned art pieces is required or recommended in a
particular situation.

(2) The term/duration of the consignment agreement should
be specified. If the agreement is to span some years, the term
of agreement clause should be tied into an "early termination" provision which would describe the specific circumstances under which either the artist or the gallery may
terminate the agreement. If the term of the contract is contingent on sales of the gallery or productivity of the artist,
those provisions should also be spelled out.

(3) Whether the gallery may assign its rights under the
contract should be discussed. At the very least, any right to
assign under the contract should be contingent on giving
prior written notice to the artist.

(4) Gallery cash disbursement items which should be covered
in the contract include the costs of promotion and the
opening night reception. The contract should state specifically whether the artist or the gallery will be responsible
for such costs.

(5) The scope of the consignment or representation agreement should be as specific as possible. If the contract is an

"exclusive," then the nature of the exclusive representation should be spelled out, detailing exactly what the artist may or may not do in the gallery's "territory."

(6) Transportation, storage and insurance provisions should be as specific as possible, leaving no doubt about who pays for what, who bears the risk of loss under given situations, and when the gallery is required to consult with the artist regarding insurance coverage and insurance valuation.

(7) Artistic control should be an important consideration. Questions such as reproduction in books and magazines, inclusion in group and travelling shows, and artist approval of sales, should be thoroughly discussed.

(8) The various exclusive rights of copyright ownership should be studied by legal counsel so that appropriate provisions may be made for transfers of those rights in consignment and other artistic property exploitation contracts. For example, if the gallery is to have some discretion in the reproduction of an art work in its possession on consignment, the contract should spell out a procedure for obtaining prior approval by the artist for such reproduction. The artist and his attorney should also be consulted about any language appearing on the commercial documents used by the gallery in sales of the artist's work, so that the bundle of exclusive rights are not transferred by contract with transfer of the "material object."

(9) Selling prices should also be determined in the contract. Issues such as periodic review, auctions, or discounting procedures, renting in lieu of sale, and billing procedures, should be stated in the contract.

(10) In exclusive representation contracts, the issue of artist income from sources other than the gallery should be discussed. This would include the right of the artist to make private sales, and the disposition of income derived from contests and awards, rentals, lecture fees, and the like.

(11) Accounting and payment procedures should be as spe-

cific as possible, as should the provisions relating to advances and guarantees. Since this area is the source of great anxiety for many artists, it is best to discuss and resolve these matters at the very beginning of the gallery relationship.

(12) Other considerations include: the confidentiality of both gallery and artist mailing lists; resale royalty rights of the artist; availability of arbitration if there is a dispute between the artist and the gallery over a material matter in the contract; the gallery's right to visit the author's studio; the artist's say regarding gifts and exchanges involving his work; inventory and recordkeeping procedures and access of the artist to such documents; the artist's control over exhibitions of his work outside of the gallery; and sale warranties and certificates of authenticity.

This by no means exhausts the possible subjects which could be covered in a well drafted consignment agreement involving the visual arts. Each situation requires its own special analysis and customized contract.

"Form contracts" are rarely appropriate in defining the complicated relationships formed between artists and galleries. When trouble arises, these "forms" often fail to provide clear guidance—unless the parties have sat down well in advance of signing the contract, discussed each and every item of the form, and amended it to fit their particular needs. Artists and galleries do themselves a disservice if they sign but do not read, and customize their written contracts.

Sales of Artistic Properties
The 1976 Copyright Act reversed the previously established expectation that a copyright is automatically conveyed with the purchase of an art work. According to the Act, the *owner of a copyright* (that is, the artist) has the exclusive right to reproduce and to authorize others to reproduce the copyrighted work; and to distribute copies to the public by sale or other transfer of ownership, or by rental, lease, or by lending.[98] Further, transfer of ownership of an art work does not

in itself convey any rights to the receiver of that work. Thus, when a copyrighted oil painting is sold, the copyright remains with the artist. Unless otherwise agreed to in writing, the oil painting owner *does not* own the copyright, nor may he or she reproduce it or authorize others to copy it, without permission of the artist.[99]

The assumption under prior law that transfer of a piece of art work automatically guaranteed ownership of the copyright prompted the development of several contract forms reserving copyright ownership for the artist.[100] The so-called Projansky-Sieglaub Contract[101] was a response to many of the unfavorable aspects of prior copyright law.

The "sales" contract for works of art involves matters or warranties of authenticity and edition;[102] disclosures of various sorts;[103] and in states with fine art prints laws, the issue of fraud. The artist contemplating the disposition of works of art by sale or lease should keep the following "legal" matters in mind:[104]

(1) *Gallery Sales Documents:* The artist and his or her attorney should insist that the gallery consult with them in preparing commercial documents used in sales or other dispositions of the art work. This is to insure that the rights reserved for the artist by the 1976 Act are not inadvertently transferred.

(2) *Recording:* If the sale of a piece of art work also includes transfer of ownership of one or all of the exclusive bundle of copyrights, it is advisable to record the documents with the Copyright Office.

(3) *Publication:* In selling the right to reproduce his or her art work in a magazine or other publication, the artist should insist that a separate copyright notice accompany his or her work. This will insure that any missing copyright notice which is the fault of the publisher does not impinge upon or erode any of the artist's copyright claims, and also serves as a reminder that the artist's copyright claims are reserved.

(4) *Resale Royalties:* Depending on the bargaining power of

the individual artist, the possiblity of reserving the right to receive royalties if there are future sales is a point to include in a "sales agreement." As will be discussed later, in California, under certain circumstances, the artist is automatically entitled to such resale royalties.

(5) *Loans:* If the artist hopes to reserve the right to "borrow" his work for future exhibitions, an agreement should be worked out with the purchaser at the time of sale. Terms and conditions governing such borrowings should be as specific as possible, covering insurance, risk of loss, storage and transportation, and ownership credits.

Once again, this is only a sampling of the issues to consider when there is a sale, lease, or other disposition of a work of art.

MISCELLANEOUS LEGAL TOPICS

Besides the law of copyrights and contracts, there are a host of other legal topics which apply to visual arts laws.

Tort and Constitutional Law Considerations

A "tort" may be defined as the commission or omission of an act by a person, the result of which is injury, whether direct or indirect, to another person's property or reputation. Among the "torts" of interest to the visual artist are those of defamation, and invasion of the right to privacy.

"Defamation" is the tort of injuring a person's reputation, character, fame, esteem, respect, goodwill, or confidence, by the utterance of derogatory, false and malicious statements in public. A defamatory "written" statement is "libelous," while an oral defamatory statement is "slanderous." An artist who displays a work which tends to diminish the esteem, respect and reputation of a person engages in the publication of a "libel."[105] An alleged libelous statement by an artist may be either a conditional privilege because it is a statement about a matter of social interest, or a matter of fair comment or criticism, either of which is a possible defense in a libel lawsuit. Although there are no strict guidelines for the artist, a guide to follow in such matters is reasonableness and good taste.

Another tort of interest to the artist is the tort of invasion of the "right to privacy." Unlike the tort of defamation, the person whose alleged "right to privacy" has been violated need not show that the publication of the art piece constituted the utterance of a "falsehood."[106] Basically, the right to privacy may be characterized as the "right to be let alone," a right violated by unwanted pubicity. Under certain circumstances, some people, such as "public figures," give up some of their right to privacy, but even they may not necessarily be fair game for the artist or anyone else.[107]

The constitutional issue of freedom of speech as guaranteed by the First Amendment to the Constitution, and the limitation on that right by the imposition of criminal penalties for acts of "obscenity," is a complicated topic which deserves more detailed attention than may be given here.[108] In general though, laws may be enforced which outlaw the display of patently sexual materials which represent or describe ultimate sexual acts, or acts of masturbation, excretory functions, and lewd and outrageous exhibition of the genital organs. Once again, there are no strict guidelines for the artist, other than to use restraint and exhibit good taste. Moreover, a piece of art work considered to be "obscene" in a small farming community may not be considered obscene in a large cosmopolitan area.[109]

Tax Laws
There are many special tax problem areas of interest to the artist[110], some of which are briefly mentioned here:

(1) For expenses to be deductible business expenses,[111] they must be incurred while the artist is engaged in a trade or business which generates a profit.[112] Rules and regulations under federal tax laws determine whether the activities of an artist may be defined as "business or trade," the expenses of which qualify for tax deductions. If it is decided that an artist

is engaged in a "hobby," then the expenses are personal and not deductible.

(2) Except in very narrow cases, prizes and awards such as those won in juried exhibitions must be included in calculations of gross income.[113]

(3) When an artist makes a charitable contribution of one of his works, the amount of the charitable contribution for tax purposes is based on the cost of the materials used to produce the work.[114]

Proper tax planning is particularly important because of the unfavorable treatment of art that has appreciated in value in the estates of artists, and the various gift tax consequences which apply to certain transfers of work. There are also advantages associated with formation of corporations by artists and art organizations; and very special rules relate to the acquisition and maintenance of tax-exempt status[115] for not-for-profit art institutions.[116] Once again, early consultation with a professional person n.ay help to ease the tax burden of the artist and his or her estate.

State Laws Affecting Artists

New York and California have been particularly active in the area of arts legislation.[117] California's *droit de suite* resale royalty legislation has recently been held to be constitutional by a United States District Court,[118] and New York has been in the forefront in passing legislation protecting the art consuming public[119] and the artist in artist/gallery relations.[120]

Droit de suite is a concept first developed under French law, by which an artist and his or her heirs have an inalienable right to share in the resale proceeds of works of art sold through a dealer or by auction within 50 years of the death of the artist. This concept has been embraced by several countries, but has not been recognized by statute on the federal level in the United States. Only California has adopted legislation in the area.[121] Under Section 986 of the California Civil

Code, whenever a work of fine art is sold by other than private sale, the artist is entitled to a 5 percent royalty. The legislation only applies to works of art with gross sale prices over $1,000.

Fine art print legislation has also been passed in Illinois,[122] California,[123] and New York.[124] Under the Illinois law, for example, when fine art prints are sold at retail or wholesale for more than $50 unframed or $60 framed, the commercial documents documenting the sale must disclose the name of the artist and the year the work was printed. This applies whether the print is an etching, engraving, woodcut, lithograph, or whether the seller does not know what kind of print it is. The commercial documents must also contain information regarding trial proofs, edition, the existence or destruction of the plate, and the name of the workshop, if any, which printed the edition. The law exempts prints sold by the artist directly to a consumer.

Droit Moral

The doctrine of the "moral rights" of the artist is another concept generally embraced in the United States. The doctrine provides that an artist has, among other rights, (1) the right to have his or her name associated with his or her work; (2) the right to modify and correct his or her work even if it is in the hands of a purchaser, (3) the right to withdraw work after publication or display to the public, (4) the right to prevent others from claiming credit for the work, and (5) the right to prevent others from incorrectly attributing authorship to the artist.[125] Though many of these rights are not generally recognized in the United States, some may be secured by contract, and recently a congressional bill was introduced which would amend the copyright law "to secure the rights of authors of pictorial, graphic, or sculptural works to prevent distortion, mutilation, or other alteration of such works . . . "[126]

—Clarence S. Wilson, Jr.

Notes

1. *See, e.g.,* Reif, *Auction Houses Say Boom Continues,* N.Y. Times, July 1, 1979, §1, at 30, col. 1. Also see *Wall Street Journal,* July 16, 1979, at 15, col. 3 ("Art Investment and IBM").

2. Mutual funds and other syndications for the purchase of art have become popular with some investors. These high-risk investments are loaded with disclosure problems. Maidenberg, *A Risky Way to Buy Collectibles,* N.Y. Times, June 3, 1979, §3, at 2, col. 2. *Generally, see* L. DUBOFF, THE DESK BOOK OF ART LAW 361 (1st ed. 1977) [hereinafter cited as DUBOFF].

3. For an early case which wrestled with the distinction between art and non-art, *see Brancusi v. United States,* T.D. 43063, 54 TRES. DEC. 428 (1928), where the Customs Court decided that Constantine Brancusi's "Bird in Space" sculpture could be brought into the United States duty-free as art.

4. *See,* Fishman, "The Emergence of Art Law," 26 CLEV. ST. L. REV. 481 (1977).

5. Symposia, 26 CLEV. ST. L. R. 479 (1977), 27 HASTINGS L. J. 951 (1976), 4 ENVIRONMENTAL LAW 461 (1974), 10 CONN. L. REV. 545 (1978); B. BURNHAM, THE ARTS CRISIS (1975); D. COCHRANE, THIS BUSINESS OF ART (1978); CRAWFORD, LEGAL GUIDE FOR THE VISUAL ARTIST (1977); Weil, Art and the Law, 70 L. LIB. J. 1 (1971); L. ADAMS, ART ON TRIAL: FROM WHISTLER TO ROTHKO (1976); J. MERRYMAN & A. ELSEN, LAW, ETHICS AND THE VISUAL ARTS: CASES AND MATERIALS.

For an excellent earlier legal sourcebook, *see* F. FELDMAN & S. WEIL, LEGAL AND BUSINESS PROBLEMS OF ARTISTS, ART GALLERIES AND MUSEUMS (1973) (Practicing Law Institute).

6. 17 U.S.C. app. §§101-810 (1976) (effective date Jan. 1, 1978). The 1909 Copyright Act, as amended to the passage of the 1976 Act, is found at 17 U.S.C. §§1-216 (1976).

7. For a thorough discussion of the subject under English law, *see* Karlen, "What is Art? A Sketch For A Legal Definition" 94 L.Q. REV. 383 (1978). *Also see,* "Art Law; What is Art Law?," NEW YORK LAW JOURNAL, Jan. 21, 1976, at 1, col. 1; at 3, col. 1.

8. 37 C. F. R. §202.3(b) (iii) (1978).

9. 17 U.S.C. app. §§101-810 (1976), P.L. 94-553, 90 Stat. 2541 (Oct. 19, 1976). The 1909 Act may be found at 17 U.S.C. §1 *et seq.* (1976). On copyright law *generally, see* NIMMER ON COPYRIGHT (1978), and Marke, United States Copyright Revision and Its Legislative History, 70 L. LIB. J. 121 (1977) [hereinafter cited as "Marke"].

10. 8 Anne, ch. 19 (1710).

11. Report of the Senate Committee on the Judiciary, 94th Cong., 1st Sess., Calendar No. 460, Senate Rept. 94-473 (1973). *Also see,* Conference Report, 94th Cong. 2d Sess., House Report 94-1733 (1976); Report of the House Committee on the Judiciary, 94th Cong., 2d Sess., House Report 94-1476 (1976).

12. Marke, *supra* note 9, at 125.

13. Studies prepared for the Subcommittee on Patents, Trademarks, and Copyrights of the Committee on the Judiciary, United States Senate, which may be of interest are: "The History of the U.S.A. Copyright Law Revision from 1901 to 1954" (Study #1) (STUDIES 1-4 (1960)); "The Moral Right of the Author" (Study #4) (Studies 1-4 (1960)).

14. Copyright law is a branch of the law of "intellectual property."

15. *See* legislative reports accompanying Public Law 94-553, *supra* note 10.

16. *See generally,* PRACTICING UNDER THE COPYRIGHT LAW OF 1976 (1978) (Practising Law Institute); Symposium on the New Copyright Law at the 1977 Meeting of the American Bar Association. 25 BULL. CR. SOC. 191 (1978). *Also see,*

CRAWFORD, THE VISUAL ARTIST'S GUIDE TO THE NEW COPYRIGHT LAW (1978) (63 page laymen's language guide to the subject), [1978] COPYRIGHT L. REP. (CCH).

17. 17 U.S.C. app. §101 (1976) (definitions).

18. *Id.*

19. 17 U.S.C. app. §301 (1976).

20. 17 U.S.C. app. 301 (b) (1976).

21. 17 U.S.C. app. §§302, 303, 304 and 305 (1976).

22. Works copyrighted before 1978 and in their first term under the 1909 Act on January 1, 1978 (e.g., works copyrighted between Jan. 1, 1950, and December 31, 1977). The 1976 Act provides that these works are entitled to copyright protection for 28 years, with a renewal term of 47 years.

23. 17 U.S.C. app. §302 (1976).

24. 17 U.S.C. app. §305 (1976).

25. 17 U.S.C. app. §303 (1976).

26. *Id.*

27. 17 U.S.C. app. §304 (1976).

28. 17 U.S.C. app. §305 (1976) provides that terminal date calculations for this purpose " . . . run to the end of the calendar year in which they would otherwise expire."

29. 17 U.S.C. app. §102(a) (5) and (6) (1976). The 1909 Act enumerated 14 classes of copyrightable works; among those included are works of art, reproductions of art works, photographs, prints and pictorial illustrations including prints or labels used for articles of merchandise.

30. 17 U.S.C. app. §102(b).

31. 17 U.S.C. app. §101 (1976) (definitions).

32. As tenants in common in regard to the rights obtaining in the copyright, it is advisable where possible to create written agreements between the joint authors about how the copyright is to be disposed of under any given set of circumstances.

33. 17 U.S.C. app. §101 (1976) (definitions).

34. *Id.*

35. 17 U.S.C. app. §201(c) (1976).

36. 17 U.S.C. app. §104(b) (1976). Sovereign authorities of treaty nations and stateless persons are also protected.

37. 17 U.S.C. app. §104(a) (1976).

38. 17 U.S.C. app. §201(a) (1976).

39. *Generally see,* Weisbond, "Highlights of Ownership and Transfer Provisions of the New Copyright Law," 25 BULL. CR. SOC. 221 (1978); Note, Transfer of Copyrights For Security Under the New Copyright Act, 88 Yale L.J. 125 (1978); Rothenberg, Oral Copyright Contracts and the Statute of Frauds, 25 BULL. CR. SOC. 159 (1977).

40. 17 U.S.C. app. §201(d) (1976).

41. 17 U.S.C. app. §201(d) (2) (1976).

42. 17 U.S.C. app. §201(b) (1976). A "work made for hire" is defined in 17 U.S.C. app. §101 (1976) (definitions).

43. 17 U.S.C. app. §101 (1976) (definitions).

44. 17 U.S.C. app. §204(a) (1976).

45. 17 U.S.C. app. §204(b) (1976) provides that a certificate of acknowledgement, though not required, is prima facie evidence of the execution of the transfer.

46. 17 U.S.C. app. §205(a) (1976).

47. 17 U.S.C. app. §205(c) (1976).

48. 17 U.S.C. app. §205(d) (1976).

49. 17 U.S.C. app. §203 (1976).

50. 17 U.S.C. app. §203(a) (3) (1976).

51. 17 U.S.C. app. §203(a) (4) (1976).

52. 17 U.S.C. app.§304(c) (1976). On the subject matter *generally, see* Curtis, "Caveat Emptor in Copyright: A Practical Guide to the Termination-of-Transfers Provisions of the New Copyright Code," 25 BULL. CR. SOC. 19 (1977).

53. 17 U.S.C. app.§106 (1976).

54. 17 U.S.C. app.§101 (1976) (definitions).

55. *Id. Also see,* Note, "Burden of Proving First Sale Under the Copyright Act of 1976," 67 GEO. L.J. 293 (1978); *American International Pictures, Inc.* v. *Foreman,* 576 F. 2d 661 (5th Cir. 1978).

56. 17 U.S.C. app.§101 (1976) (definitions).

57. 17 U.S.C. app.§107 (1976).

58. 17 U.S.C. app.§108 (1976).

59. 17 U.S.C. app.§101 (1976) (definitions). *See,* Gottlieb and Nolen, "Pictorial, Graphic and Sculptural Works Under the New Act," in CURRENT DEVELOPMENTS IN COPYRIGHT LAW 501 (1977) (Practising Law Institute).

60. 17 U.S.C. app.§102(5) (1976).

61. *See* Circular Rlc published by the Copyright Office. *Also see,* "Works of art (Class G) of works registrable with the Copyright Office," 37 C.F.R.§202.10 (1978).

62. 17 U.S.C. app.§102 (1976) (subject matter of copyright).

63. 17 U.S.C. app.§113 (1976).

64. *See,* Oppenheimer, Originality in Art Reproductions: "Variations" in Search of Theme, 26 BULL. CR. Soc. 1 (1978).

65. *Mazer* v. *Stein,* 347 U.S. 201 (1954).

66. 17 U.S.C. app.§101 (1976) (definitions).

67. 17 U.S.C. app.§113(b) and (c) (1976).

68. H.R. 2706, The Design Protection Act of 1979, introduced on March 7, 1979, by Illinois Representative Thomas R. Railsback.

69. *See, e.g., Pushman* v. *N.Y. Graphic Society,* 287 N.Y. 302, 39 N.E. 2d 249 (1942).

70. 17. U.S.C. app.§202 (1976).

71. *Id.*

72. 17 U.S.C. app.§109(b) (1976). Ownership is required in order for the possessor of the material object of the copyright to exercise Section 109(a) and (b) rights. Consequently, a person in possession of a material object by rental, lease, loan or otherwise is not the owner for the purposes above, 17 U.S.C. §109(c) (1976).

74. 17 U.S.C. app.§401(a) (1976).

75. See, e.g., *Letter Edged in Black Press, Inc.* v. *Building Commission of Chicago,* 320 F. Supp. 1303 (N.D. Ill. 1970) (the Picasso sculpture in Chicago's Civic Center is held to be in the public domain because maquettes of it had been published without the requisite copyright notice).

76. 17 U.S.C. app.§101 (1976) (definitions).

77 17 U.S.C. app.§401(b) (1976).

78. 17 U.S.C. app.§401(c) (1976).

79. 42 Fed. Reg. 64374 (Dec. 23, 1977).

80. 17 U.S.C. app.§405 (1976).

81. 17 U.S.C. app.§406 (1976).

82. 17 U.S.C. app.§405(c) (1976).

83. 17 U.S.C. app.§407, 408, 411, 412, 301 (1976).

84. 17 U.S.C. app.§407 (1976).

85. 37 C.F.R. §202.21 (1978).

86. 37 C.F.R. §202.20(c) (2) (iv) (1978).

87. 37 C.F.R. §202.20(c) (2) (viii) (1978).

88. 37 C.F.R. §202.20(d) (1978).

89. *See,* Circular R30. A particularly useful kit for attorneys is made available through the Copyright Office. It contains all the forms and Circulars, copies of the

Act and legislative history, and copies of bills introduced in the Congress which would affect copyright law.

90. 17 U.S.C. app.§501-510 (1976). *Also see, Gross v. Seligman,* 212 F.2d 930 (2d Cir. 1914); *Miller Brewing Co. v. Carling O'Keefe Breweries of Canada, Ltd.,* 452 F. Supp. 429 (W.D. N.Y. 1978); *Franklin Mint Corp. v. National Wildlife Art Exchange, Inc. and Ralph H. Stewart,* [1978] COPYRIGHT L. REP. ¶ 25,004 (3d Cir., April 17, 1978) (Nos. 77-1527 & 77-1526).

91. 17 U.S.C. app.§506 (1978).

92. RESTATEMENT OF CONTRACTS §1 (1932).

93. *See, e.g.,* ILL. REV. STAT., ch. 59, §§1, 2, 9, 10, and the UNIFORM COMMERCIAL CODE Statute of Frauds provisions.

94. An excellent collection of art and entertainment related contracts may be found at 2 A. LINDEY, ENTERTAINMENT, PUBLISHING AND THE ARTS (1963 and Supp. 1977).

95. Lynes, "The Artist as Uneconomic Man," SATURDAY REVIEW, Feb. 28, 1970, at 25; Rosenbaum, Artist-Gallery Contracts—Scenes From a Marriage, 65 ART IN AMERICA 10 (July/August, 1977).

96. *See, e.g.* F. FELDMAN & S. WEIL, LEGAL AND BUSINESS PROBLEMS OF ARTISTS, ART GALLERIES AND MUSEUMS 463 (1973) (Practising Law Institute); Weiner, "The Artist and His Gallery," 2 PERFORMING ARTS REVIEW 91, 107 (1971).

97. *In re Estate of Rothko,* 43 N.Y. 2d 305, 401 N.Y.S. 2d 449 (1977). *Also see, In the Matter of Friedman,* 64 A.D. 2d 70, 407 N.Y.S. 2d 999 (N.Y.A.D. 1978). Much has been written on the *Rothko* case, *see, e.g.,* SELDES, THE LEGACY OF MARK ROTHKO (1978) (the author was a journalist who covered the litigation involving the Rothko estate).

98. 17 U.S.C. app.§106 (1976).

99. 17 U.S.C. app.§202 (1976).

100. *See* 5 AM. JUR. LEGAL FORMS 2d §72:251 et seq. (1971); 2 RABKIN & JOHNSON, CURRENT LEGAL FORMS §4.42A (1978).

101. The contract is entitled an "Agreement of Original Transfer of Work of Art;" and it is reproduced in L. DUBOFF, THE DESK BOOK OF ART LAW 1131 (1st ed. 1977).

102. Feldman, "New Protection for the Art Collector—Warranties, Opinions, and Disclaimers," 23 RECORD 661 (1968); Comment, "Uniform Commercial Code Warranty Provisions and the Theory of Strict Liability in Tort as Solutions to Art Counterfeiting in Painting: A Critical Analysis," 20 ST. LOUIS U.L.J. 531 (1976); Section 219-c of the General Business Law of New York; R. DUFFY, ART LAW: REPRESENTING ARTISTS, DEALERS, AND COLLECTORS 13-55 (1977) (Practicing Law Institute).

103. Duffy, "Disclosure Requirements in Connection With The Sale of Fine Arts Prints," 48 CALIF. S.B.J. 528 (1973).

104. Other "contract issues" include: insurance contracts, Pfeffer, Insuring Museum Exhibitions, 27 HASTINGS L.J. 1123 (1j976); contests, Annot., "Private Rights and Remedies Growing Out of Prize-Winning Contests," 87 A.L.R. 2d 649 (1963); insurance, DUBOFF, *supra* note 2, at 477; auctions, DUBOFF, *supra* note 2, at 537; DuBoff, Auction Problems: Going, Going, Gone, 26 CLEV. ST. L.R. 499 (1977).

105. *See,* Note, "Defamation, Privacy and the First Amendment," 1976 DUKE L.J. 1016 (1976).

106. The "right of privacy" was first identified as an independent right in Warren and Brandeis, The Right to Privacy, 4 HARV. L. REV. 193 (1890).

107. The landmark decision in the area is *New York Times v. Sullivan,* 376 U.S. 254 (1964). *See* the latest pronouncements on "public figure" status by the

Supreme Court in *Wolston* v. *Reader's Digest Association, Inc.,* 47 LAW WEEK 4840 (1979).

108. *Roth* v. *United States,* 354 U.S. 476 (1957) signalled the modern test of obscenity as " . . . whether to the average person, applying contemporary community standards, the dominant theme of the material taken as a whole appeals to prurient interest." The *Roth* obscenity test has given way to various "community standards" definitions by which a piece of art work or literature is to be judged.

110. *Generally, see, COLLECTORS AND ARTISTS: PLANNING AND PROBATING THE ESTATE* (R. Lerner, ed. 1978) (Practising Law Institute); Behrenfeld, Coming Into Their Own—Identifying and Planning For the Emerging Taxable Estate, 36 N.Y.U. INST. FED. TAXATION 231 (1978); Darling, Estate Planning: Planning for the Exotic Assets: Hobbies, Collections, Oil and Gas Interests, Horses, Dogs, etc., 35 N.Y.U. INST. FED. TAXATION 1227 (1977); Clark, Fine Art: Administering This Valuable Estate Asset, 117 TRUSTS & ESTATES 132 (1978); Echter, Equitable Treatment for the Artist's Estate: The Tax Court Takes a First Step, 114 TRUSTS & ESTATES 394 (1975); O'Connell, Defending Art Valuations For Tax Purposes, 115 TRUSTS & ESTATES 604 (1976); Beghe, Artist, the Art Market and the Income Tax, 29 TAX. L. REV. 491 (1974); TAX ANGLES IN PATENTS-TRADE-MARKS-COPYRIGHTS (1978) (CCH Editorial Staff Publication).

111. I.R.C. §162.

112. I.R.C. §183(b).

113. I.R.C. §74(b) excepts prizes and awards made primarily in recognition of religious, charitable, scientific, educational, artistic, literary, or civic achievement, when the recipient was selected without any action on his or her part, and is not required to render substantial future services as a condition to receiving the prize or award. In this category would be cash grants such as the Nobel Prize.

114. I.R.C. §170(e). The latest legislation introduced in the 96th Congress which would establish more equitable bases upon which the value of artistic property for such situations may be judged, is H.R. 1847 (Rep. Jack Edwards) and H.R. 2498 (Rep. Abner J. Mikva). *Also see,* H.R. REP. NO. 1515, 94th Cong. 2d Sess. (1976).

115. I.R.C. §501(c) (3).

116. Symposium, Nonprofit Arts Institutions, 10 CONN. L. REV. 545 (1978); Skindrud, Recognition Under Section 501(c) (3) of the Internal Revenue Code as a Prerequisite to Arts Grants: A Special Problem For Literary Publishers and Art Galleries, 26 CLEV. ST. L. REV. 529 (1977).

117. Katz, "Copyright Preemption Under the Copyright Act of 1976: The Case of Droit de Suite," 47 GEO. WASH. L. REV. 200 (1978) discusses the possible preemption of California's artists' royalties legislation because droit de suite legislation speaks to an economic interest not the purview of state action because of Section 301 of the 1976 Act.

118. *Moresburg* v. *Balyon et al.,* [1979] COPYRIGHT REP. ¶ 25,077 (C.D. Cal., March 23, 1978).

119. N.Y. GEN. BUS. LAW §219-c (McKinney Supp. 1979).

120. N.Y. GEN. BUS. LAW §219-a (McKinney Supp. 1979). *Also see,* Comment, "Regulation of the New York Art Market: Has the Legislature Painted Dealers Into a Corner," 46 FORDHAM L. REV. 939 (1978).

121. *See generally,* Solomon and Gill, Federal and State Resale Royalty Legislation: "What Hath Art Wrought?", 26 U.C.L.A. L. REV. 322 (1978); Schulder, "Art Proceeds Act: A Study of the Droit de Suite and a Proposed Enactment For the United States," 61 NW. U. L. REV. 19 (1966); Duffy, "Royalties for Visual Artists," 11 J. BEVERLY HILLS B.A. 27 (1977); Price, "Government Policy and Economic Security for Artists: The Case for the Droit de Suite," 77 YALE L. J. 1333 (1968); Ashley, Critical Comment on California's Droit de Suite, Civil Code Section 986, 29 HASTINGS L. J. 249 (1977).

122. ILL. REV. STAT., ch. 121 1/2, §§361-369 (1977).

123. CAL. CIV. CODE §§1740-1745 (West's Comp. ed. 1979).

124. N.Y. GEN BUS. LAW §228, and Reg. 30 of New York City's Consumer Protection Law.

125. *See generally,* Merrymen, "The Refrigerator of Bernard Buffet," 27 HASTINGS L. J. 1023 (1976); Comment, "The Doctrine of Moral Right: A Study of the Law of Artists, Authors, and Creators," 53 HARV. L. REV. 554 (1946); Comment, "Artist's Personal Rights in His Creative Works: Beyond the Human Cannonball and the Flying Circus," 9 PACIFIC L. J. 855 (1978); *Vargas* v. *Esquire, Inc.,* 164 F. 2d 522 (7th Cir. 1948); *Gilliam* v. *American Broadcasting Co.,* 538 F. 2d 14 (2d Cir. 1976).

126. H.R.288, "Visual Artists Moral Rights Amendment of 1979," introduced by Representative Robert Drinan on January 15, 1979.

Income Tax and Record Keeping for the Individual Artist

Whatever the aesthetic concerns of the artist, he or she is also running a business. Like any other businessperson, he or she is responsible for keeping books and records from which income tax returns may be prepared. Additionally, since these records measure monetary performance, they may also be used to show artist/business persons "how they did" financially.

The first determination to make is whether the artist is carrying on a business or pursuing their art as a hobby.

Business vs. Hobby

A business is a pursuit carried on for livelihood or for profit. For a pursuit to be recognized as a business, a profit motive must be present and some type of economic activity must be involved.

You may be a full time employee of another business and at the same time be engaged in one or more business activities on your own. In order to deduct business expenses, you should be able to demonstrate annually by facts and circumstances that you are, indeed, engaged in business.

An activity is considered a business if it is entered into and carried on in good faith for the purpose of making a profit. Thus a profit making activity (a business) must be distinguished from an activity engaged in purely for self-satisfaction.

Two characteristic elements of a business are regularity of

activities and transactions and the production of income. If, in a given year, no income or a small amount of income is coupled with expenditures that produce a loss, there may be a question whether a business was carried on in that year.

Other important factors entering into this determination are:

a. Attendance at or matriculation from an art school;
b. Membership in professional art organizations;
c. Recognition by the community or by professional peers;
d. Continuing education in the particular artistic field.

The absence of income in itself does not prevent you from deducting the ordinary and necessary expenses directly connected with or pertaining to an activity that constitutes your trade, business, or profession.

Generally, a profit motivation is presumed if the activity produces a profit in any two of five consecutive years, unless the Internal Revenue Service establishes the contrary.

Business Organization

A business may be organized as a sole proprietorship, a partnership (for two or more owners), or as a corporation. Each type of organization has advantages and disadvantages and the choice is important, so professional guidance should first be obtained from an attorney or a certified public accountant.

Choosing an Accounting Method

The two basic accounting methods are the cash and accrual methods.

Under the cash method revenues are reported when actually or constructively received and expenses are reported when actually paid. Under the accrual method, revenues are reported when the right to receive them is earned and expenses are deducted when incurred rather than when paid.

Although the accrual method is the accepted method for financial reporting, artists should usually adopt the cash method because of its simplicity and because its emphasis on the reporting of income and expense is sufficient for income tax requirements.

Record Keeping

You must keep records to determine your correct tax liability. Regardless of your bookkeeping system, your records must be *permanent, accurate, complete,* and must clearly establish income and deductions. The law does not require any particular kind of records.

Double-entry bookkeeping, a system which records assets and liabilities as well as income and expense, is ordinarily preferable for most businesses. However, single entry bookkeeping which records only income and expenses is simpler and sufficient for the business which does not have a large number of financial transactions. In most cases the single entry method should be used by the artist.

To begin with, *you should deposit all business receipts in a separate bank account and establish a petty cash fund for small expenses.* All business expenses paid by cash should be supported by documents that clearly show they are for business purposes.

Make all disbursements by check if possible, so that business expenses may be well documented. Checks made payable to yourself should be limited to appropriate withdrawals of income from your business. Checks made payable to cash should be avoided. This will help you to distinguish between disbursements made for business purposes and disbursements that are attributable to income withdrawn from your business.

If you must write a check payable to cash or to yourself to pay a business expense by cash, include the receipt for the cash payment in your records. If you cannot get a receipt for a cash payment, you should make an adequate explanation in your records at the time of payment.

Cancelled checks, paid bills, duplicate deposit slips, and other documents that substantiate entries in your records should be filed in an orderly manner and stored in a safe place. Memorandums or sketchy records that merely approximate income, deductions, or other pertinent items affecting your tax liability will not be considered adequate. If a petty cash fund is not used, petty cash expenditures should be documented in a diary.

At the end of each month (or more often depending on the level of activity), revenues and expenses should be recorded in appropriate journals and reconciled to bank balances. At the end of the year, all journals should be summarized and the totals reconciled to bank balances.

MONTHLY CASH RECEIPTS JOURNAL

Date	Source	Sale	Owner's Draw	Deposited in Bank
Jan. 5	Sam Small	$ 100	100	—
Jan. 8	Percival	50	—	—
Jan. 12	Alice Tully	80		80
Jan. 20	Tom Levin	97	60	37
Jan. 25	John Swift	140	70	70
Jan. 28	Joe Tolve	724		724
	Totals	$1,191	$230	$961

The Monthly Cash Receipts Journal summarizes revenue activity for the month. It also identifies the source of the revenue and the amount of such revenues deposited in the bank or retained by the owner.

The journal totals are carried forward to an annual revenue summary. The total bank deposit is used to reconcile cash at the end of each month.

This journal summarizes all checks issued in the month. The journal is balanced by totalling all columns except the "amount of check" column. This total should equal the total in the "amount of check" column.

The monthly journal totals are carried forward to an annual disbursement summary. The "amount of check" total is used to reconcile cash at the end of each month.

MONTHLY CHECK DISBURSEMENTS JOURNAL

Date	Payee	Check No.	Amount of Check	Materials and Supplies	Utilities	Office	Owner's Draw	General Account	Amount
Jan. 4	Smith	101	$100	$100					
Jan. 6	Con Ed	102	60		$60				
Jan. 12	Smith	103	200				$200		
Jan. 16	Smith	104	200				200		
Jan. 18	Ma Bell	105	40					Telephone,	$40
Jan. 21	O.S. Co.	106	80			$80			
Jan. 22	U.S.P.O.	107	100					Postage,	100
			$780	$100	$60	$80	$400		$140

MONTHLY CASH RECONCILIATION
1/31

Balance on bank statement			$ 746
Add—deposit in transit—1/28			724
Total			1,470
Deduct checks outstanding	105	$ 40	
	106	80	
	107	100	220
Adjusted balance per bank statement			$1,250
Balance per checkbook 1/1			$1,069
Add—deposits (per cash receipts journal)			961
Total			2,030
Less—disbursements			
(per check disbursements journal)			780
Checkbook balance 1/1			$1,250

ANNUAL SUMMARIES

Cash Receipts

Month	Sales	Owner's Draw	Deposited in Bank
January	$ 1,191	230	961
February	1,220	220	1,000
March	1,416	410	1,006
April	1,524	500	1,024
May	1,620	200	1,420
June	3,240		3,240
July	1,824	24	1,800
August	2,814	400	2,414
September	1,642	200	1,442
October	1,690	300	1,390
November	1,870	200	1,670
December	2,040	40	2,000
	$22,091	$2,724	$19,367

CHECK DISBURSEMENTS

Month	Total Disbursed	Materials and Supplies	Utilities	Office	Owner's Draw	Telephone	Postage	Auto	Miscellaneous
January	$ 780	$ 100	$ 60	$ 80	$ 400	$ 40	$ 100	$—	$—
February	1,600	600	100	90	300	90	80	240	100
March	800								
April	1,350								
May	1,540								
June	3,160								
July	1,650								
August	1,890								
September	1,560								
October	1,840								
November	1,950								
December	810								
Totals	$18,930	$3,550	$1,400	$1,780	$8,000	$1,600	$800	$1,400	$400

ANNUAL CASH RECONCILIATION
12/31

Balance per bank statement	$ 1,740
Deduct checks outstanding—	
896 $ 52	
897 74	
898 108	234
Adjusted balance per bank statement	$ 1,506
Cash in bank 1/1/__	$1,069
Total bank deposits	
per the annual recent summary	19,367
Total	20,436
Less—total check disbursements	
per the disbursements summary	18,930
Cash in bank—12/31/__	$ 1,506

Using the types of journals, summaries and reconciliations shown here will usually be sufficient to provide the data needed to properly prepare income tax returns.

Other Records

In addition to the ͨͨsh receipt and disbursement records, the artist/business-person will have out-of-pocket expenditures to control and summarize in order to arrive at net business income.

Record keeping rules for travel and entertainment are as follows:

Elements to be Substantiated (1)	For expenditures for travel away from home (2)	For expenditures for entertainment (3)
Amount	Amount of each separate expenditure for transportation, lodging and meals. Permissible to aggregate incidental expenses in reasonable categories, such as gasoline and oil, taxi fare, daily meals for traveler, etc.	Amount of each separate expenditure. Incidental items such as taxi fare, telephones, etc. may be aggregated on a daily basis.
Time	Dates of departure and return for each trip, and number of days attributable to business activities.	Date of entertainment or use of a facility for entertainment. (Duration of business discussion.)
Place	Destination by name of city or other appropriate designation.	Name and address or similar designation of place of entertainment, or place of use of a facility in connection with entertainment. Type of entertainment if not otherwise apparent. (Place of business discussion.)
Business Purpose	Business reason for travel or nature of business benefit derived or expected to be derived.	Business reason or nature of business benefit derived or expected to be derived. Nature of business discussion or activity if entertainment is other than "business only".

Business Relationship   Not applicable.

Occupations or other occupation— such as names or other designations—about persons entertained which establishes their business relationship to taxpayer. (Identification of persons entertained who participated in business discussion.)

Record keeping rules:

Travel expenses:

Date:	Item:	Place:	Amount:	*Business Purpose:*
April 1	Air fare (round trip Chicago-Dallas)	Dallas	$111.20	Drama workshop
	Lunch and tip		4.20	
	Lodging		18.50	
April 2	Meals and tip		6.50	
	Auto rental (2 days)		22.00	
	Tips		1.50	

Entertainment expenses:

Date:	Item:	Place:	Amount:	*Business Purpose:*	*Business Relationship:*
April 1	Dinner and tip	Ajax Grill, Dallas	$16.50	Discuss contract	Director

In addition to the documentation required to substantiate travel, entertainment and other out-of-pocket expenses, all of these expenditures should be summarized monthly by category in a manner similar to the annual check disbursements summary.

Since many artists use their personal residences to carry on their art businesses, it is important to know the rules for taking a business-at-home deduction. The premises used must be:

1. The principal place of business, or

2. The place of business used to meet clients, etc. in the normal course of business, or

3. A separate structure used in connection with the trade or business.

The business portion of the premises must be used *exclusively* for business and on a *regular* basis. A portion of a dwelling unit that is used for both personal purposes and for carrying on a trade or business does not meet the exclusive use test.

Explanation of Entries on Schedule C

(1) The cash method of accounting should be adopted in the first year a Schedule C is filed. Consequently, sales represent *collections* for the year for sales of artwork.

(2) From the "Annual Cash Receipts Summary".

(3) From the "Annual Check Disbursements Summary".

(4) Cost of operations to the artist is essentially the purchase of supplies used in the creation of artwork. Since unused supplies are not significant in relationship to the annual results of operations, they are not inventoried.

(5) Owner's draw is considered to be a distribution of net business income and thus is not allowed as a deduction in the determination of net business income.

(6) Total auto expenses per "Annual Check
Disbursements Summary" $1,400
Less portion deemed to be personal use—20%   280
Business portion $1,120

The "actual" method of determining auto expense has been used here. Another method is the standard mileage method. Under this method a deduction is allowed of $.17 a mile for the first 15,000 miles of business use and $.10 a mile thereafter. The standard mileage rate may be used in one year, changed to actual the next, and then changed back to using the standard mileage rate the next year. Its use is limited to individuals not using more than one car simultaneously in their business or employment. You must, however:

a) Own the car;

b) Not use the car for hire, such as for a taxi;

d) Not operate a fleet of cars using two or more simultaneously;

d) Not have claimed depreciation using any method other than one straight-line method; and

e) Not have claimed additional first-year depreciation on the car or truck.

If your car is fully depreciated, or is considered to be fully depreciated under the straight-line method, you may deduct only 10c a mile for all miles of business use.

(7) Depreciation is computed in Schedule C-2. You may deduct each year, as depreciation, a reasonable allowance for the exhaustion, wear and tear, and obsolescence of depreciable property used in your trade or business or held for the production of income. This enables you to recover your cost or other basis of depreciable property during its estimated useful life. Depreciation is computed on the basis of the business property. However, the basis for nonbusiness property converted to business use is its fair market value on the date you begin using it in your business, or the adjusted basis of the property at that time, whichever is less. There are several methods of computing depreciation, but the easiest is straight-line which is shown here.

(8) Deductions for out-of-pocket expenses. The journal summarizing such expenditures is not reproduced here.

(9) In this example we are assuming that Mr. Brown rents a 5-room apartment for $500 per month. One of these rooms is

used exclusively for carrying on his business. He may therefore deduct 20% of his annual rent.

(10) Uncollected amounts for sales of artwork are not deductible as bad debts since such amounts were never included in income under the cash method of accounting. The lost "cost" attributable to such uncollected amounts has been deducted since all material expenditures are deducted in the year paid.

Albert S. Kaplan, C.P.A.
(Partner, Shepard, Schwartz & Harris)

SCHEDULE C	**Profit or (Loss) From Business or Profession**	
(Form 1040)	(Sole Proprietorship)	**1978**
Department of the Treasury	Partnerships, Joint Ventures, etc., Must File Form 1065.	
Internal Revenue Service	▶ Attach to Form 1040. ▶ See Instructions for Schedule C (Form 1040).	

Name of proprietor	Social security number of proprietor
HARRY BROWN	345 : 22 : 6263

A Main business activity (see Instructions) ▶ _Artist_ ; product ▶ _Original artwork_

B Business name ▶ _Harry Brown_

C Employer identification number ▶ _NONE_

D Business address (number and street) ▶ _1215 Center Street_ **C**

City, State and ZIP code ▶ _Wilmette, Illinois 60015_

E Accounting method: (1) ☒ Cash (1) (2) ☐ Accrual (3) ☐ Other (specify) ▶

F Method(s) used to value closing inventory: _Does not apply_

(1) ☐ Cost (2) ☐ Lower of cost or market (3) ☐ Other (if other, attach explanation)

	Yes	No
G Was there any major change in determining quantities, costs, or valuations between opening and closing inventory? . . If "Yes," attach explanation. _Does not apply_		
H Does this business activity involve oil or gas, movies or video tapes, or leasing personal (section 1245) property to others? (See page 25 of the Instructions.)		X
I Did you deduct expenses for an office in your home?	X	

Part I Income

1 a Gross receipts or sales . . . . (2) . .	**1a**	22,091			
b Returns and allowances	**1b**				
c Balance (subtract line 1b from line 1a)			**1c**	22,091	
2 Cost of goods sold and/or operations (Schedule C–1, line 8)			**2**	3,550	
3 Gross profit (subtract line 2 from line 1c)			**3**	18,541	
4 Other income (attach schedule)			**4**	–	
5 Total income (add lines 3 and 4) . . . . ▶			**5**	18,541	

Part II Deductions

6 Advertising			**28** Telephone	1,600	(3)
7 Amortization			**29** Travel and entertainment . . .	500	(8)
8 Bad debts from sales or services .	–	(10)	**30** Utilities	1,400	(3)
9 Bank charges			**31 a** Wages . . . (5)		
10 Car and truck expenses	1,120	(6)	**b** New Jobs Credit . .		
11 Commissions			**c** Subtract line 31b from 31a .		
12 Depletion			**32** Other expenses (specify):		
13 Depreciation (explain in Schedule			**a** Miscellaneous	400	(3)
C–2)	1,454	(7)	**b** Cab fare	74	(8)
14 Dues and publications	40	(8)	**c**		
15 Employee benefit programs . . .			**d**		
16 Freight (not included on Schedule			**e**		
C–1)			**f**		
17 Insurance			**g**		
18 Interest on business indebtedness			**h**		
19 Laundry and cleaning			**i**		
20 Legal and professional services .			**j**		
21 Office supplies	1,780	(3)	**k**		
22 Pension and profit-sharing plans .			**l**		
23 Postage	800	(3)	**m**		
24 Rent on business property . . .	1,200	(9)	**n**		
25 Repairs			**o**		
26 Supplies (not included on Schedule C–1) . .			**p**		
27 Taxes			**q**		
			r		

33 Total deductions (add amounts in columns for lines 6 through 32r) . . . . ▶	**33**	10,368	
34 Net profit or (loss) (subtract line 33 from line 5). Enter here and on Form 1040, line 13. ALSO enter on Schedule SE (Form 1040), line 5a. (For "at risk" provisions, see page 25 of Instructions.) . . . . ▶	**34**	8,173	

Schedule C (Form 1040) 1978   **Page 2**

SCHEDULE C–1.—Cost of Goods Sold and/or Operations (See Schedule C Instructions for Part I, Line 2)

1 Inventory at beginning of year (if different from last year's closing inventory, attach explanation) .	**1**	DNA
2 a Purchases **2a**		
b Cost of items withdrawn for personal use **2b**		
c Balance (subtract line 2b from line 2a)	**2c**	
3 Cost of labor (do not include salary paid to yourself)	**3**	
4 Materials and supplies . . . . (3) .	**4**	3,550
5 Other costs (attach schedule)	**5**	
6 Add lines 1, 2c, and 3 through 5	**6**	3,550
7 Inventory at end of year	**7**	DNA
8 Cost of goods sold and/or operations (subtract line 7 from line 6). Enter here and on Part I, line 2 . ▶	**8**	3,550 (4)

SCHEDULE C–2.—Depreciation (See Schedule C Instructions for line 13)
If you need more space, please use Form 4562.

Description of property (a)	Date acquired (b)	Cost or other basis (c)	Depreciation allowed or allowable in prior years (d)	Method of computing depreciation (e)	Life or rate (f)	Depreciation for this year (g)
1 Total additional first-year depreciation (do not include in items below)————————▶						
2 Other depreciation:						
Buildings						
Furniture and fixtures	1/15/77	1,200	180	S.L.	10 yr	120
Transportation equipment . .	1/01/77	4,000*	1,667	S.L.	3 yr	1,667
Machinery and other equipment .	Less – personal use –	20%				333
Other (Specify) _____	Business portion					1,334
*Net of $3,000 salvage value						
	5,200					1,454

3 Totals **3**   1,454

4 Depreciation claimed in Schedule C–1 . . . .   **4**   –

5 **Balance** (subtract line 4 from line 3). Enter here and on Part II, line 13 . . . . ▶   **5**   1,454

SCHEDULE C–3.—Expense Account Information (See Schedule C Instructions for Schedule C–3)

Enter information for yourself and your five highest paid employees. In determining the five highest paid employees, add expense account allowances to the salaries and wages. However, you don't have to provide the information for any employee for whom the combined amount is less than $25,000, or for yourself if your expense account allowance plus line 1, page 1, is less than $25,000.

Name (a)	Expense account (b)	Salaries and Wages (c)
Owner		
1		
2		
3		
4		
5		

Did you claim a deduction for expenses connected with:	Yes	No
A Entertainment facility (boat, resort, ranch, etc.)?		
B Living accommodations (except employees on business)?		
C Employees' families at conventions or meetings?		
If "Yes," were any of these conventions or meetings outside the U.S. or its possessions? (See page 26 of Instructions) .		
D Vacations for employees or their families not reported on Form W–2?		

☆ U.S. GOVERNMENT PRINTING OFFICE: 1978-0-263-313 E.I #36-2890346

A Guide to Real Estate
for the Artist

A SHORT, CURSORY, WHOLLY INADEQUATE, YET NEVERTHELESS ENGAGING, OVERVIEW OF REAL ESTATE LAW

Real estate is dirt. Yet, it is also a building over a thousand feet tall providing living and working space for tens of thousands of people and a small wooden shack housing indifferently either a power transformer or a vagrant; it is the continent of Africa and that frugal patch of earth on which you grow carrots; it is a sandy coastal plain under millions of tons of ocean and it is that oft-scarred bit of rock that climbers poke their flags into at the top of a mountain. But to the law it is a sub-species of the genus "property."

What property is is disputed. It is not mixtures of different types of matter—these are things which may be reduced to property. Rather, property is an idea that has taken shape in many theories of social organization. It has been variously described as an objectification of force or power giving rise to wealth and political and social privileges; an inalienable, natural right common to all peoples (of acquisitive temperament); outright theft and an undermining of the commonweal; and governmental largesse channelled through statutorily constructed conduits to specified classes of beneficiaries. But perhaps the most useful way to understand property is as a creature of law which takes its form from the law and cannot exist without the law.

The law distinguishes two broad classes of property, real and personal, and recognizes in an owner of property a certain bundle of rights which can be localized in a person or other entity, can be separated one from another and can be transferred from one owner to another. Although *real property* is generally thought of as land it is also everything that is naturally a part of the land (such as a forest or a mineral deposit so long as the trees and ore remain attached to the earth) and those things which are more or less permanently attached to it. *Personal property* is all property other than real property and it includes such items as different from one another as the copyright to an epic poem, stock certificates evidencing ownership of a multinational corporation, and a lumpy sofa. The distinction between real and personal property is important because the legal rules which apply to how title may be transferred, how it may be inherited, and how it might be pledged as collateral for a loan are often different for each.

Ownership: What Kind and How
Of all things one can do with and to property, owning or possessing it are the primary concerns of real estate law. Owning and possessing property are not the same although they are closely related. Owning real estate allows one to use it, to keep others from using it and to get rid of it. Possession of real estate is limited to the physical control of the land or improvements. In some instances, where possession is held "adversely" by one not the owner against one who is, possession may eventually ripen into ownership.

What one owns after receiving an interest in real estate is not always the same. The most complete interest the law recognizes is called the *fee simple*. This interest gives one ownership of the real estate itself and everything below it (i.e. mineral rights) and everything above it (i.e. air rights) in perpetuity. Most states now have laws that dictate that when a document purporting to convey an interest in real estate does not specify what type of interest is being conveyed, it is presumed to be a fee simple. It is possible to fracture the fee in several ways involving two characteristics of ownership: what is owned and for how long.

Separate elements of the fee, such as the mineral rights or air rights, can be sold or leased without relinquishing ownership of the land surface. It is also possible to allow another the limited use of one's real estate interest by granting an easement. Perhaps the most familiar type of easements are rights-of-way for streets or public utility services, but there is a wide variety ranging from the right to graze one's cows in another's pasture to the right to bury one's relatives in a common cemetery. There are a number of technical distinctions which apply to easements and which separate them from similar interests such as licenses and "profits," but the important feature of any easement is that it is not an ephemeral privilege but an interest in real estate that is granted in a written document, which may be recorded, lasts forever, unless otherwise specified, and allows a specific, limited use of a parcel of land.

Ownership of the entire fee can be sold or otherwise "alienated" (i.e. gotten rid of) for some length of time only to return to the original owner or his heirs at some point in the future. A life estate accomplishes this by granting someone ownership for his or her life (or for that matter any specified person's lifetime) and providing for the shifting of ownership interest when the life has ended. One who has a life estate is a "life tenant" and one to whom the ownership will shift when the life estate has ended is a "remainderman." A life tenant may do whatever he wishes with his interest—even sell it (although the market may be limited if he is old or sick). A remainderman can only sit and fret unless he can establish that his life tenant has done or not done something which has substantially diminished the value of the property. Various forms of trusts today have largely supplanted the life estate as a method of conveying title to real property, but it is still prevalent enough to induce the Internal Revenue Service to propagate elaborate rules about evaluating its worth.

Other time-limited real estate interests are the estate or term for years (better known to the hapless renter as a lease which is discussed later in some detail), the tenancy at will or by sufferance, and future estates and interests. A true tenancy at will is one where the duration of the real estate interest depends solely upon the mutual desires of the lessor and lessee. Under such and arrangement a lessee might move at any time without notice to the lessor and without liability to pay any rent which may accrue after his departure. Likewise, a lessor may take legal action to remove the lessee without notice. Laws in nearly every state have mitigated the abruptness of this rough and ready remnant of the common-law by requiring that notice of termination of tenancy be given in writing. A tenant by sufferance is one who lawfully enters into possession but stays on after his legal right to remain and his welcome have expired. Statutes generally regulate notice requirements and money damage consequences in this case as well.

The phrase "future interest", simple and innocuous though it may seem to the uninitiated, has chilled the blood and frazzled the nerves of uncounted generations of law students. It denotes various methods of conveying title to real estate which for all their complexity, inconsistency, and archaic elegance have defied both tractability and extinction for several hundred years. Simply stated, a future interest is a right to obtain possession of property at some time in the future or upon the occurence of some future event. The remainder following a life estate is a future interest and it may be "vested" or "contingent"—vested if the remainderman ("remainderperson" does not yet seem to have found its way into legal literature) is certain to receive the property at the end of the life estate or contingent if his receiving the property is predicated on some condition which may or may not exist at the time the life estate ends. A "reversion" occurs when the right to possession reverts back to the person (or his heirs) who has granted it after some period of time has elapsed or some specified event has taken place. Such events are often phrased in terms of "limitations" or "conditions." If an event automatically expunges a right to possession, it is a limitation; if the grantor of possession must also step in and take affirmative action to cut off possession, the event is a condition generally referred to as a "condition subsequent." As arrid and abstruse as these distinctions might seem, they still are commonly encountered in the form of restrictions on land limiting its use to single family dwellings or a church or a school or preventing alcohol from being served on it. Some restrictions are illegal and unenforceable because they are against public policy or unconstitutional, e.g. racial restrictions.

Whatever interest in real estate is involved, there are several ways of acquiring it. One can either receive a government grant of land, take title by deed, inherit by will or the laws of intestacy, or squat obnoxiously and continuously for a specified period of time. (The so-called "inchoate" rights of wife's dower, under which a widow is entitled to a one-third interest for life only in real estate owned by her husband during their marriage, and husband's curtesy, under which the husband has a life interest in his wife's real estate provided the marriage has produced an heir capable of inheriting this real estate, have been so extensively and variously modified by different states that it is impossible to discuss them in general terms.)

Government land grants are usually made by documents called "patents" which are filed or recorded. Unless fraud of one sort or another can be established, a land patent is conclusively presumed to be evidence of good title. Much of the land in the United States has the origin of its chain of title in a government land grant. Perhaps the most common method of acquiring title to land today is the deed. Deeds are always written instruments containing a very specific description of the land and a statement that the named grantor is transferring his interest in the land to the named grantee. When one wishes to make a gift of an interest in land after death, the most common technique is a will setting out the details. Such a gift is a "devise" and its validity is governed by the laws dictating the requirements of a will in the state where the land is located and not necessarily where the testator lived—unless a reciprocity statute is in effect. If there is no will, or if the will is invalid, title to all property, including real estate, passes to the decedent's heirs in the proportion set out by state law. Adverse possession is a much more adventuresome idea. Briefly stated, it is that if one, without a scintilla of right to be there, trespasses openly and notoriously on another's land for a continuous and lengthy period of time (usually fifteen or twenty years), he will be awarded, for his brazen cunning, title to the real estate while the original owner will be punished for his lack of vigilance by losing all of his rights to the land—however long he may have held them or however much he may have paid for them. Enticing as this route to ownership may seem, adverse possession is not a very practical method of acquiring title. One of the reasons is that the statutory period of time which must run before title can change hands stops running if the original owner or owners is a minor or an incompetent and does not start running again until this disability is removed making the validity of any title acquired sometimes uncertain.

How title to real estate is held can be just as important as what interest is held or how it was acquired. There are several ways in which title can be held, but perhaps the simplest is either in one's own name or that of a nominee. Where only one owner is involved and where proper estate planning has been done, this is generally an adequate method and is used frequently. Where more than one owner is involved, there are several co-ownership devices that are often used. One is *tenancy in common* in which one co-owner's death will cause his interest in the property to pass to his heirs, or whomever he designates in his will. This differs from a *joint tenancy* where a co-owner's death will pass his interest to the remaining co-owners. Because public policy no longer favors creation of joint tenancies among unmarried individuals, most states have laws which provide that where no specific type of tenancy is created in a conveyance of title to multiple owners, tenancy in common will be presumed. However, if property is conveyed to a married couple without specifying how they are to take title, a *tenancy by the entirety* is generally created—it has the same effect as a joint tenancy. A joint tenancy will be converted into tenancy in common if one of the joint tenants grants his interest to a third party. The new owner will hold title as a tenant in common with his co-owners.

Married individuals' property rights are governed by the concepts of community property or local divorce laws depending upon where they live. In those states which have community property legislation, all property acquired by either spouse during the marriage is generally considered to belong to both equally. Unmarried couples living together currently have uncertain property rights. Litigation in different states has not conclusively determined whether the law will compel sharing of property and several states have proposed laws which would solve the problem in different ways. At the moment, a written ante-coital agreement or chastity seem the most prudent approaches.

In those real estate transactions involving commercial property which is held for income or tax shelter purposes, "entity" title holding devices are preferred. These are basically the corporation, partnership, land trust, and real estate investment trust. A *corporation* is a distinct legal entity chartered under the laws of a state, run on a day-to-day basis by its officers, managed by its directors, and owned by its shareholders. It can make automobiles, sell tortillas or, among many other things, own real estate. It offers the advantages of limited liability (in the event something goes wrong, a shareholder's liability is usually, although not always, limited to his investment in the corporation) and flexibility (ownership of the real estate can be split up and constantly shifted among different individuals by simply changing the number of shares each owns). On the other hand, its start-up costs, formality (e.g., officers, directors, meetings, annual reports, franchise and capital stock taxes), and tax ramifications make it unsuitable for most title holding purposes.

Partnerships are more popular. They are distinct legal entities as well, but they are not charted by a state and are governed usually by written partnership agreements drawn up by the parties involved (although recklessness and naivete sometimes produce oral partnership arrangements) and state law which is in most states an adoption of the Uniform Partnership Act. Although in the ordinary partnership liability extends to all of the personal assets of the partners, this is not the case for the most used real estate investment vehicle, the *limited partnership*. In a limited partnership there are two classes of partners: general and limited. The general partner manages the affairs of the partnership and has personal liability for any problems, financial or otherwise, which arise. The limited partner's liability is limited to his investment in the partnership, but he cannot actively participate in its management. One of the most attractive features of the partnership, and one that distinguishes it from the corporation, is that any income it has or loss it sustains is passed through, for tax purposes, to its partners. A corporation's income or loss stays with it and does not trickle down directly to its shareholders. (It should be noted that Subchapter S of the Internal Revenue Code, if elected by a corporation, will allow it to be treated in most respects as a partnership for tax purposes. However, the limitations on the availability of this election often make it unsuitable for larger real estate investments.) Because commercial real estate developments often have high initial expenses and little income, they generate losses which, in a partnership, can be used to offset or "shelter" other income of the investing partners.

Land trusts exist in several states as a result of special legislation. These devices enable a trustee (usually a bank but not necessarily so) to hold the legal title to real estate while any number of beneficiaries hold the beneficial interest in the trust. The device allows the flexibility of splitting ownership among many individuals in different proportions and easily shifting these interests without most of the disadvantages of the corporate entity. A land trust also provides a degree of anonymity to the "real" owners because only the identity of the trustee appears on conveyancing documentation. *Real estate investment trusts* are creations of the Internal Revenue

Code which allow large number of investors to pool their resources for the purpose of acquiring one or more real estate developments. If the requirements of the Code are met, the investment entity is treated as a corporation for tax purposes.

Buying and Selling:
Points to Ponder (Weak and Weary)
Few things done sitting down give as much satisfaction as buying or selling a parcel of real estate. For the buyer, there is a feeling of accomplishment in possessing something substantial and immortal; for the seller, there is either a feeling of elation at having capitalized on a good investment or relief at having gotten away with the money and experience to do better the next time. For both sets of these expectations to be met, there are a number of things both parties should be aware of in documenting any real estate transaction.

The first is that any real estate transaction should be documented—in writing. Although it is certainly legal for one to hand a sack of money over to someone in simultaneous exchange for a deed to land, this is seldom prudent. The law has for the past several hundred years required an agreement for the sale of land to be in writing if it is to be enforceable. This writing is the contract for sale and it is the blueprint which outlines and organizes the entire transaction. Preparation of this contract is the most critical step in any deal because mistakes or omissions in it are nearly always impossible to remedy later.

Unless the seller intends to participate in financing the buyer's purchase in one form or another, he is generally only interested in receiving one thing from the deal: money. This fact suggests a fundamental principle of contract drafting: a short agreement will favor the seller and a longer one the buyer. The buyer must live with the deal's consequences in a way that requires warranties and representations the contract should provide. Whatever the length of the document, there are a number of provisions it should contain. It should begin by specifying who the parties to the deal are and at which addresses they can be contacted. This is not as simple as it seems. The seller(s) must be everyone who has an interest in the property; the buyer(s) everyone who intends to acquire an interest. Where individuals are involved, their marital status should be specified and spouses should be named. Next the property to be sold should be described in detail. This description should include the "legal description" which is an elaborate exposition of lot and block numbers or a metes and bounds narration reminiscent of a pirate's treasure map and a physical description actually describing the improvements on the parcel and its dimensions. Just after the real estate is reduced to print, a list of the personal property included in the sale should be inserted. The results of the disputes over chandeliers and refrigerators down through the years could fill a blood bank. The parties should agree and note in their contract exactly what the buyer is getting and what the seller is keeping.

Obviously, a very important term of the contract is the price to be paid. Not so obviously, the price as listed is seldom the price paid. Even in the case of a cash deal for a small bungalow where no financing is involved, there are often "prorations" or adjustments to the price made at closing for credits that might be extended to the seller (e.g. for prepaid insurance premiums) or the buyer (e.g. for a prior year's taxes accrued but not billed). The contract should make whatever price is specified subject to such prorations as the most convenient method of settlement at closing. The price itself is often the least ambiguous term of the agreement—but not always. It is one thing to purchase a summer home for forty thousand dollars—it is another to purchase several acres of vacant industrial property for seven dollars a square foot. In the later case, a survey made by a competent surveyor attached to the contract and detailing the exact number of square feet involved may save a great deal of trouble.

Once the price is noted the manner of paying it should be discussed. It is possible, though not fashionable, to make a lump sum cash payment. Actually, one of the major attractions of real estate investment is the "leveraging" effect one can obtain by borrowing funds to make a purchase. Traditionally, it has been relatively easy for borrowers to obtain financing for the majority of the purchase price of real estate because lenders can secure their loans conspicuously and regard real estate as good collateral. As a result, nearly every purchase of land involves financing of one sort or another. The financing may come from the seller or from a third party. If the seller agrees to finance the sale, he may do so by either accepting a purchase money mortgage or entering into an installment sales arrangement with the buyer. In the former case, he simply substitutes for a bank. The buyer receives a deed at closing and makes mortgage payments to the seller. Under the latter agreement, the buyer generally does not receive a deed at closing but rather acquires title only after all of the payments have been made. The essential difference, although this may vary with the jurisdiction, is that in the event of non-payment a buyer has generally greater rights under a mortgage than under an installment contract.

Whatever the source of the financing, a deposit will nearly always be required at the time the contract is signed. Contracts usually provide this deposit will be forfeited to the seller if the buyer defaults and does not complete the purchase. Therefore, sellers would like as large and buyers as small an earnest money deposit as possible. The amount is a matter to be negotiated between the parties but whatever it is should be specified in their contract. Where a buyer will require financing to complete the purchase, his ability to procure it on terms acceptable to him should be made a condition to his obligation to close the deal. The condition clause should state the minimum amount of the loan the buyer will require and term of years to repay it and the maximum interest rate and loan fee (or "points" usually expressed as a per centage of the amount borrowed) he will agree to pay. If financing cannot be obtained on these terms, a properly drafted condition clause will allow the buyer to recover his deposit and escape the deal.

In the pile of papers the buyer receives at closing, one stands out in importance: the deed. A buyer will always receive a deed (unless an installment purchase is involved) to evidence the actual change in the title of the property from one party to another. The contract should specify what type of deed a buyer will receive and what, if anything, the grant of ownership it makes will remain subject to. There are warranty deeds, special or limited warranty deeds, bargain-and-sale deeds, quitclaim deeds, executor's and administrator's deed, and trustee's deeds among others. The consequence of issuing one or the other of these deeds in different states can be different. Suffice it to say that with the advent of modern title indemnity devices, the type of deed received is generally not critical. Nevertheless, a warranty deed is preferred where obtainable. There are certain types of exceptions to the grant of "full and unencumbered" title which exist in nearly every transaction and which cause no serious trouble. There are others that may cause problems. All exceptions to which the deed will be subject should be stated in the contract. These may include existing leases or tenancies, easements for utility services or rights-of-way, party wall agreements, general or special real estate taxes or any other peculiarity of the particular deal. If one or more of these exceptions is not satisfactory to the buyer (i.e. a long term low rent lease to the seller's brother-in-law for half of the premises), the difficulty should be resolved before the contract is signed or at least the contract should exclude the troublesome exception as one the deed will be made subject to in the hope the problem can be resolved before closing.

Closing is the ceremony at which title to the property usually passes in exchange for money. It is usually attended by both parties to the deal, a representative of the buyer's lender, and the real estate broker involved, if any. The contract should provide for a definite date of closing. Even if this date is not met, setting it more clearly delimits the rights of the parties in the event of a dispute. Closings are sometimes done by means of an escrow. Such an arrangement allows more flexibility in that different documents required are simply deposited with an escrowee who holds them and makes proper exchanges of paper and funds without the need for a number of people to meet. Inasmuch as escrowees generally make a charge for their services, the contract should provide that in the event an escrow is used a specified escrowee will be used and the fees will be paid in some agreed way.

If a real estate transaction is properly closed, the buyer immediately on closing receives ownership of the property. In most cases, he would also like possession and this is an issue the contract must discuss in some detail. If the seller is not to surrender "possession" at closing, some time period should be specified at the end of which possession will be transferred. If the period is to be any significant length of time, a rent and expense provision should be inserted as well. The buyer will begin to incur expenses immediately on the transfer of title (e.g. taxes, interest, insurance) even though he may not have possession. The seller should pay an equitable portion of these expenses until possession changes hands. It may be advisable to subtract some portion of the seller's proceeds at closing and establish an escrow fund to pay seller's portion of these expenses. In some instances, the term possession itself should be defined. It is fairly easy to transfer possession of a vacant acre of earth, but what about an apartment building filled with people or a garage filled with junk? Surrendering possession may mean removing the people and the junk if it is so defined and it should be if these considerations are important to the buyer.

Every contract should provide that the buyer will be given adequate title indemnity in one form or another. "Title indemnity" is simply a generic expression for any of a number of methods developed to insure the buyer that the seller in fact owns the property he purports to sell, that the title to this property is free of troublesome encumbrances, and that the buyer may rely on these representations when he purchases. Different methods of title endemnity obtain in different parts of the country, but the most common are title abstracts and opinions, title insurance and government land title registration. An abstract of title is a chronologically organized summary of the substance of documents or facts appearing on the public records and which affect the condition of title to real estate. To be of value to the buyer, it should be reviewed by an attorney who should render an opinion as to the validity of title in the seller. Title insurance streamlines this procedure slightly. A title insurance company conducts a search of the title and in a report which is known as a commitment to issue title insurance lists the persons it finds to be then in title and any "exceptions" or anomalies to clear title. Buyer's legal counsel may review this report and decide which, if any, of the exceptions are unacceptable. An attempt to have the insurance company "waive" unacceptable exceptions can then be made, which is done by producing documentation the insurer requires to reassure it concerning questions its search has raised. When the report is in satisfactory condition, the deal is closed, and, for a one time premium, the title insurer issues an insurance policy in an amount which is usually identical to the purchase price and which guarantees good title to the buyer subject to the exceptions it contains.

Land title registration, known as the Torrens system because of its invention by a premier of South Australia by that name, works on a somewhat different principle. When a parcel of land is first registered in the Torrens system, its owner is issued a certificate describing the land and indicating his ownership. All matters affecting title to that land thereafter should be noted on the face of this certificate and its duplicate in a central registration office. When the owner wishes to sell the property, he simply surrenders his certificate to the registration office which cancels it and issues a new one to the buyer. The need for title searches is eliminated because all matters affecting title should be noted on the certificate itself. Suffice it to say that this system works better in theory than it does in practice, although the economies it allows (i.e. usually smaller charges than comparable title insurance premiums) sometimes make it attractive.

Depending upon the type of real estate involved, the contract should contain certain warranties and representations made by the seller to the buyer. If the services of a real estate broker were used and a commission is due, the broker and the amount of his commission should be specified. The seller should provide buyer with an accurate plat of survey of the property sold and the contract should note this and allocate the cost as the parties agree. There should be a warranty that the property is not in violation of applicable building and zoning ordinances (or at least that no notices of violations have been received by the seller). If the buyer is purchasing the property for income purposes (e.g., an apartment building) he should insist that an accurate rent schedule, lease termination table, and expense itemization be attached to the contract as a verified exhibit. Finally, all of the parties should sign the contract. If a corporation, partnership, land trust or other entity is a party, a duly authorized representative should sign on behalf of the entity.

Leasing: Another Guide to the Perplexed
Whether one needs a garret in which to write a novel, a loft in which to paint a picture, a penthouse in which to enjoy royalties, or a cold water flat in which to brood, leasing is often the most flexible and economical way of possessing real estate for a fixed period of time. Fortunately, the law dealing with leases has passed through its stormy and eccentric adolescence, but, unfortunately, it is still stuck in a menopausal period of uncertainty and change.

That real estate interest known as the *estate for years* had its beginnings in an attempt to avoid sin without substantial inconvenience. In the Middle Ages, the Roman Church labelled interest bearing loans usorious and officially banned them. Resourceful land owners loaned tenants land instead of capital and collected rent instead of interest thus growing richer, appeasing the Church, and creating a pervasive form of social organization called feudalism. Because the law of contract had not developed significantly at this point in history, the courts viewed this transaction as a conveyance of property applying those legal principles that governed other such conveyances. One of the most important of these principles was any promise or covenant made in such a conveyance was independent of any other. In other words, once the landlord conveyed (or leased) the property to the tenant, he had done everything the law required. He was not required to repair the tenant's lodgings or replace them if they burned down. On the other hand, the tenant's obligation to pay rent was unremitting. The fact that the house he leased was destroyed by fire or his crops and stock were carried off by knights errant did not relieve him of the rental payment. As long as the lease term did not expire, the landlord could not reclaim possession (even for non-payment of rent) and the tenant could not stop rent payments (even if the landlord failed to do what he promised or the property became useless.

Over the last five hundred years, courts have begun to recognize that a tenant's position is now more like that of a futile purchaser of services than a feudal farmer. Consequently, court decisions and legislation in many states have created implied warranties of habitability running from landlord to tenant concerning the condition of the premises to be leased and have made lease covenants mutually dependent (i.e. payment of rent is dependent upon landlord's doing what he promises in the lease) in the case of leases for residential property. Exactly what the respective rights of landlord and tenant are and how far, if at all, the mutual dependence of covenants idea will be extended to commercial lease situations varies from state to state. The problem becomes particularly acute in the case of lofts which have traditionally been commercial spaces but which artists are more and more turning into working and living space.

Whatever the law may imply about landlord-tenant rights, the document which defines these most clearly and definitely is the lease itself. Many apartment leases or those for a small commercial space are printed forms propagated by local real estate boards or bar associations and, with a few (but now more frequent) exceptions, are biased in favor of the landlord. Modifying such leases or doing away with them altogether is largely a function of the tenant's bargaining power. Nevertheless, in any lease there are a number of issues which should be addressed and over which there should be some constructive discussion.

As is the case with a sales contract, the lease should also contain a detailed description of the parties and the premises. It is important to ascertain that the party representing himself as the landlord has authority to enter into the lease and holds title to the property with which the lease is concerned. Some jurisdictions limit the power of a trustee to sign a lease agreement for a long term. If the landlord is a corporation, it is important that the appropriate corporate action (usually a resolution approved by the board of directors) be taken to authorize the signing of a lease. If the landlord is a governmental entity, enabling legislation may be required to allow a valid lease to exist. These considerations are of more importance for commercial long term leases than for residential arrangements, but they can become troublesome problems if overlooked in any situation. The premises should be described in as much detail as possible. Although an apartment number may be sufficient in some instances, other situations may require a detailed drawing showing the size and configuration of the space involved.

If the tenant will require appurtenant space to make use of the space he is leasing, this should be described. Most common instances involve parking space or storage space. In commercial situations, the tenant may wish to have an option to lease space contiguous to that which he occupys at some future time. That option's terms should be spelled out in his present lease in as much detail as the landlord will accept. Another matter requiring detailed specification is the use which the tenant will put the space to: one leasing a residence may be in violation of his lease if he conducts some part of his business on the premises unless the lease specifically allows this added use. This point is especially important in a loft lease where an artist expects to both live and work in the same space.

One of the most important terms of any lease is its term, i.e. the length of time for which it gives both parties rights. Terms vary with the type of property involved and the nature of the use to which it is put. Leases for summer homes seldom are written for longer than a three month term while one railroad may lease a right-of-way to another for nine-hundred and ninety-nine years. Whatever the term, the exact date on which it begins and ends should be conspicuously noted. Inasmuch as a landlord is not obligated to renew a lease unless he agrees to, a tenant who is unsatisfied with the length of the initial term or who feels he might want to remain in the premises longer depending upon his circumstances at lease expiration time should request a renewal clause of some type. Generally, a clause giving the tenant an option to renew or not is preferred. The method of exercising this option should be described and any new terms that will apply to the lease as a whole during the renewal period (e.g., the new rent) should be specified in as much detail as possible. Where the initial term of the lease is long, a landlord may be unwilling to commit himself to a specified renewal rent. Leaving the matter up to "mutual agreement" at the time of renewal is inviting litigation. At least some reference to either the consumer price index or some other adjusting device should be made to give both parties as clear an indication as possible of what each would be getting into financially if the lease term is extended.

Where a tenant expects to remain on the premises for a long time or spend a great deal of money on immovable improvements, it may be desirable for him to consider purchasing the space he is leasing at some time in the future. An option to purchase granted to the tenant in the lease will give him this important flexibility. Any option language should state as precisely as possible how it can be exercised, at what time, and for how much. A landlord with no present intention to sell his property would be understandably reluctant to grant such an option (particularly for a specified purchase price). This reluctance may be overcome with a right of first refusal in place of a tenant option. Simply put, this right allows the tenant an option to purchase the property before anyone else can do so, but only if the landlord decides to sell it. Whichever method is selected some means of fixing a price should be described. In the case of a first refusal approach, third party offers would suggest at least an approximate price. In the straight tenant option situation, if a definite price cannot be agreed upon and indexing devices seem inadequate to measure the property's projected value, an appraisal method can be specified. The parties can pick appraisers who in turn can pick another and this set of experts can determine by consensus what should be paid at the time the option is exercised.

Rent is the lifeblood of any lease. When it stops flowing the agreement may die. How much the rent is, when it is due, when it will be considered in default, and, in some cases, how it is determined, all should be detailed. Rent may consist of several components. Where the leased space is part of a large commercial space, common expenses, such as real estate taxes and janitorial costs, may be termed "additional" rent and added on a prorated basis to each tenant's "basic" rent. Aside from the built in escalation characteristics of this rental arrangement, there is the matter of verifying it. Appropriate language giving the tenant the right to inspect the books, records, and bills of the landlord should be provided wherever a tenant is asked to pay some portion of these costs. Where a tenant is a business generating income, fair rental value of its space is often best expressed in terms of a percentage of its profits. So-called "percentage" leases usually specify a modest base rental plus a percentage of earnings (gross or net) to be paid the landlord as additional rent. This arrangement allows a new business to rent concession when it most needs it and provides an investor-landlord with the potential for a much higher return. Here a landlord will want lease language giving him the right to examine periodically the tenant's financial records. Disclaimer language should be added to indicate that despite any sharing of profits, the landlord is not a partner of the tenant. A "net" lease (more neurotic documents call themselves "net net" or even "net net net" leases) shifts some of the landlord's responsibilities over to the tenant. These are primarily the financial responsibilities of paying real estate taxes and assessments, insurance premiums and some other property carrying charges. This allows the landlord a net rental return which is easy to calculate in advance and allows the tenant larger tax deductions. Where a tenant is required to pay the whole real estate tax bill, the lease should give him the right to legally protest tax assessments.

Under the old commonlaw rule, a landlord was not responsible for the condition of the leased premises at the beginning of the term. This has been modified by court decisions and laws in various states. Nevertheless, if the space is habitable, the tenant takes possession of it on an "as is" basis. Often as an inducement to a prospective tenant, a landlord will make certain assurances about redecorating or otherwise modifying the space to suit. The lease should contain these assurances and place as specific a deadline as possible on the completion of the work. If the landlord undertakes to do such work, there should be an indemnity clause protecting the tenant from the claims of workmen and suppliers employed by the landlord. Unless otherwise agreed, a tenant's responsibility to repair leased premises is limited to keeping the premises in compliance with local building safety regulations which his use may not violate. Of course, he can do no damage to the premises beyond what would be expected in the course of normal use. The point is that general rules and commonlaw principles should not be relied upon to provide practical guides to who should fix what when something goes wrong. The lease should allocate repair responsibilities as specifically as possible. Often the less space a tenant is leasing, the fewer things he will be required to repair. Where there are common areas, such as hallways, the roof, parking areas, and stairways, the obligation to repair should rest with the landlord, but if a tenant is leasing an entire factory or store complex, it may be more appropriate to leave the repair responsibility with him.

In the absence of agreement most tenant-installed fixtures (e.g. shelves, bookcases, or electrical appliances) remain the tenant's at the expiration of the lease term—provided they are promptly removed. This is why a landlord will frequently insert in a lease that no fixtures are to be installed without his prior written consent and that if they are installed they become his at the end of the lease term. A tenant installing an elaborate customized interior in the face of such a clause may become an unwitting Santa Claus. What stays and what goes is another topic to be dealt with before the lease is signed. So is the matter of a security deposit. Where a tenant is a large business entity with a triple A credit rating renting commercial space, a landlord may forego the customary request for a security deposit, otherwise, the security deposit rivals death and taxes as an unavoidable certainty. The amount of the deposit is usually some multiple of the periodic rental. If at all possible the purpose of the security deposit should be stated in some detail and its amount related to this purpose. If it is to repair tenant damage, the type and value of the premises leased should be taken into account. If the security deposit cannot be applied to past due rent, this should be explicitly stated. In some situations (usually multiple dwelling buildings over eight units) state laws require that interest be paid on security deposits at regular intervals. Even where this is not law-required, a tenant should attempt to have such a provision in his lease together with a statement of where and how the deposit will be held. A procedure for refund of the deposit should be outlined with penalties imposed on the landlord for failure to comply with it.

All predictable expenses should be allocated in the lease. Utility, heating and insurance costs must be paid to keep the premises tenantable and secure. One party or the other must pay them and pay them on time. If not the other party should be given the right to pay them and charge the defaulting party. The matter of assignment and subleases can be important. An assignment places a new party in the place of the former tenant, i.e. whatever is left of the lease term becomes the "property" of the new assignee and the old tenant is out of the picture. A sublease is simply a lease by a tenant to yet another tenant. The old tenant remains liable in every respect to his landlord. Most lease forms prohibit any sort of assignment and sublease and give the landlord the right to arbitrarily refuse even the most wonderful assignee or sub-tenant. Different courts have responded in different ways to this attitude. Most say the landlord is entitled to be stubborn. More and more, however, are finding that the law will impose the responsibility of reasonableness on the landlord's decision. If assigning or subletting is a real possibility, a tenant should insist on "reasonableness" language in the lease itself so that a sudden change in circumstances does not prove financially disastrous.

There are literally dozens of other subjects that can be and regularly are introduced into leases from the placement of signs to condemnation awards and mortgage subordination stipulations. It is impossible to discuss even most of them in a short general discussion of the subject. Nevertheless, it is important to discuss those provisions which put "teeth" into all the others: those that deal with remedies. Unlike most contractual agreements which take a positive approach to life and seldom dwell on what might happen if one party or the other does not do what he is supposed to, leases are usually pessimistic things chock full of horrible sanctions for the hapless transgressor of their terms. As one would expect these sanctions usually apply to tenants who fail to pay rent, fail to maintain the subleases, attempt to sublet, hold over their tenancy at the end of a lease term or do any of a number of things they have agreed not to. The remedy the law provides is a suit in forcible entry and detainer—which is simply an action to recover possession from the tenant. In certain situations money damages may be asked and re-covered as well.

However, landlords often use leases to take the law into their own hands. For any event defined as a tenant default, landlord remedy clauses have provided, among other things, that the landlord may declare the lease terminated and the tenant's right to possession over; that the landlord may enter the leased premises and remove the tenant and his possessions without further formality; that the landlord may relet the premises to someone else; and that while all of the foregoing is happening, the landlord may still collect the rent from the tenant for the entire original lease term. Tenant remedies have traditionally been more limited, but there is no legal reason for this to be the case. In fact, newer lease forms do make an effort to adjust what had previously been an imbalance in landlord-tenant remedies. If a landlord defaults in his obligations (e.g. failure to provide heat or maintenance), some clauses give tenants the right to either terminate the lease and move without further rent liability or make required repairs and deduct their cost from future rent payments. Ideally, the countervailing bargaining power of the parties would insure adequate remedies on both sides. Because this is often not the case, where a tenant's informed insistence does not result in language in the lease adequate to safeguard his rights, the courts will necessarily become more active participants in lease writing after the fact.

The Government:
What It Giveth It Can Taketh Away

Because real estate has traditionally been locally owned for the most part, governmental regulations concerning it have traditionally been locally imposed. Today federal regulation of some aspects of real estate ownership is increasing rapidly and although it is usually not as important to the average owner as state and local law, it is something to be dealt with whenever a substantial parcel of real estate is developed or changes ownership. Among the more visible federal regulations are those concerning financing, interstate sales, and development. The Real Estate Settlement and Procedures Act (RESPA) and Truth-in-Lending legislation are designed to provide more information to one financing a real estate purchase. They provide for disclosure of "real" interest rates and all closing costs so that a borrower may compare competitive financing and by making the most economical decision introduce more competition into the lending industry. (Lenders and real estate professionals argue that in practice the laws simply increase costs passed on to the customer.) Interstate land sales legislation requires disclosure of a number of facts bearing upon the investment potential of undeveloped or newly developed real estate. It is designed to curb the market for swamp and desert properties. The securities laws have also been employed to regulate developer marketing techniques. Whenever a real estate development may have a significant impact on the environment (rather often), the Environmental Protection Act, in one form or another, imposes restrictions on a number of construction and location features.

Of all of the things government can do to real estate, the most drastic is to take it. It can do this through its inherent power of eminent domain which it exercises through condemnation proceedings. The power is constitutionally limited in two respects: property must be taken for "public use" and the owner must be given "just compensation" for it. The actual taking is effected through a court hearing procedure most often and for those who dispute either the public use or just compensation criteria there is an opportunity to be heard. The amount to be awarded is generally based upon the testimony of expert witnesses as to the market value of the property taken although if only a part of one's land is taken compensation is also awarded for the diminution in value of what is left. When the money award is made, it steps into the shoes of the land as far as anyone with an interest in the land is concerned. In other words, the owner can receive nothing until taxes, mortgages, judgments and other liens against the property have been paid. Unless a tenant has waived all rights to proceeds of a condemnation award in his lease, he too will share in some part of them.

Particularly in urban areas, it quickly becomes apparent that there is no such thing as absolute ownership of real estate which would allow an owner to do with his property as he chooses. Refineries are not built next to school houses and stockyards are not built near high rise apartment buildings because their owners have acute aesthetic sensibilities but because the local government has acted to forbid it—usually by enacting a comprehensive code of land use regulations called a zoning ordinance. Zoning is designed to regulate land use and sometimes to enforce a comprehensive plan of community development as well. It dictates the type of uses that may be made of land in a particular area of the community. The intent is generally to segregate heavy industrial or commercial uses from primarily residential and recreational uses by specifying what kinds of buildings can be built and what can be done inside and around them in designated areas of the city or county. Since this type of regulation is considered a purely local matter, one who is dissatisfied with the manner in which his property is zoned must first take his case to an administrative review board. Appeal to the courts is possible if the board's decision is disputed. Zoning is generally the culprit preventing the widespread use of old industrial loft space in some cities for artists' workshops and residences. Some ordinances were specifically designed to prevent just what the artist has in mind—working and living in the same space. New York City is one community which has acted to change this state of affairs with new legislation and other cities where the problem has come up will probably follow suit.

Conclusion

Real estate can be an absorbing subject of scholarly research, the basis for a profitable business, the source of a feeling of comfort and security, an interesting hobby, a prudent investment, or the cause of financial disaster. Having some understanding of the law that governs real estate transactions can help avoid disaster but it cannot guarantee it. One with a little knowledge uses it properly when he understands its limitations and seeks help when he needs it.

Vincent J. Tolve

Financial Management, Budgeting, and Bookkeeping

Arts organizations hoping to reach a point of self-sufficiency and stability must have good financial management to provide them with a clear and current picture of their financial situation. It is critical for arts organizations to know where their money is being spent, which of their activities are generating profits and which are losing money, how much cash is going to be needed by the organization during its off-season, etc. These questions are possibly even more important for arts organizations, which are usually borderline economic activities with far less room for error, than for-profit businesses. Yet arts organizations have been terribly negligent in this area. I sometimes feel that this negligence is in part an over-reaction to the prevailing materialism in this country and the tendency to ignore everything but the "bottom line"; and the fear that to succeed is to "sell out." Whatever the reasons, the fact remains that the arts have historically had poor financial management.

In the arts, and with nonprofit organizations as a whole, there is a potential conflict between profit motives and art or service activities. In most business there is no such division —the business provides a good or a service in order to make money. In the arts, one must not only provide the goods and services, but be able to attract other resources in the form of grants and contributions to make it possible for the primary activity to continue. It is rare for one person to produce good art and to be a promoter as well. Arts organizations too, are inclined to be good at one or the other. Hence, it is common to find poor art which is well promoted and economically successful, and good art which is poorly promoted and unsuccessful.

Financial management in the arts poses some unique problems. Taking a hard look at the finances of an arts organization involves assigning an economic value to activities, to work, and to people. Not only are the standards which one must use to assign value to a product or to an artist's work unclear, but there are a considerable number of non-economic considerations which can enter into the picture. An arts organization can exist for its least profitable activity, and all of the other activities which on paper may look like they are the most profitable, may only be justified internally because they make it possible to do some work which is not remunerative.

In any event, it is necessary to assign a dollar value to activities, to work, and to people in an arts organization. It is also essential to ask some crucial questions of the organization—to determine what activities are central to it and its continued existence, and which activities exist to support these primary activities. This is a process of self-definition, which most of us resist to the death, but one which is necessary to determine which programs may be marginal and uneconomic, and which are central or profitable.

Budgeting

Budgeting is both an analytical and historical activity, and a predictive one. By the time a budget is actually created, these aspects are combined into a plan of action for the coming financial period. For an on-going operation it is common to simply take the figures for the previous year—the revenues and the expenditures—and to estimate what the percentage of increase or decrease will be for the various items, and then to insert these new figures into the budget for the coming year. This process, known as *incremental* or *step budgeting,* is perfectly adequate if your organization's plan is in full tilt, if the economic situation is stable, and the organization is in good financial shape. It does not entail asking basic questions, though, and usually fails to analyze the exact position of individual organizational activities. Step-budgeting implies a continuation of policy decisions that took place at some time in the past.

A more hard-headed approach—though one that is also more time consuming—is to require that every activity justify itself both financially and in terms of the goals of the organization. This type of budgeting, known as *zero-based budgeting*, is rigorous and potentially disquieting to an organization. The implicit question that is asked is "prove that this activity is worth supporting." Though it is time-consuming and unsettling, few arts organizations are in a position not to ask this question on a regular basis.

Personnel costs in the arts are high, so it is desirable to begin your zero-based budget by allocating staff time to activities, to figure out how much employee time is devoted to each of the programs of the organization. A distinction should be drawn between the activities for which the organization exists, and those activities which sustain these primary activities. A simplified *Program Budget* is drawn up in Illustrations I and II.

Program Budgets are useful for determining how much different programs cost, and for determining how much "support" these activities require. Looking at Illustrations I and II, we can see that the Peacock Players would be operating with a $5,600 deficit for 1978. A closer look at the budget reveals that of the three primary activities, the school is the least profitable, operating at a loss of $7,200. In analyzing the budget, the directors of the Peacock Players might decide that the school is not an essential part of the program of the organization, and that it is desirable to eliminate it, thereby balancing the budget. The directors might feel that the school was capable of generating more revenue, and that an intensive promotional campaign for the school which would cost $500 could generate another $10,000 in revenues, thereby justifying its existence. On the other hand, the directors could decide that the school was not profitable, but that it was an essential part of the organization because the majority of the actors and actresses in the company were trained at the school. In the last instance it would be necessary to draw up a new budget which would attempt to alleviate the projected deficit in another way. Zero-based budgeting is not a decision-making process in itself, but it frequently presents financial information in a new light, which then facilitates decision-making.

The same analysis should be applied to the major productions planned for the coming season—as well as to those of the previous seasons—to determine which plays will be generating and which will be losing money, and to justify each of the program choices. Though in this instance we are talking about theatre, the same principles would apply to any other programmed arts activity.

A major dilemma for many arts organizations is how to deal with a deficit budget. Historically, arts organizations have tended to be a bit schizophrenic on the subject, operating as though there was no way of altering the projected program—so that all costs tended to be thought of as fixed—and defending this position against critics by calling on such shibboleths as "artistic freedom." All the while hoping that some "angel" would step in at the last moment and magically make up the deficit with one grand flourish of the checkbook. Clearly this is not a reasonable way to exist in a world where there have never been many, and are now fewer and fewer, such beneficent angels. All of this is not to say that you shouldn't take risks, but that you should know when you are taking them and be prepared to suffer the consequences. Take comfort in the words of one seasoned arts administrator who confesses, "Since I went back into the 'culture business', I do nothing else from five in the morning, when I wake up sweating with anxiety, till I go into a troubled sleep, than think about money" (John Houseman, *Producers on Producing*).

In addition to program budgets and a general operating budget, it is desirable for most organizations to draw up a *Cash Budget*. The function of this budget is to give the administration an idea of when they are going to actually have the money that they will be spending in the course of the year. If all revenues were to come in at the first of the year and could be allocated over the next twelve months when bills came due, there would be no problem. This is rarely the case, and it is in fact more common for revenue such as grants and donations to come in after the close of the financial year. There may be several periods in the course of the year when most of the revenue comes in, for example with schools where tuition is due at the beginning of each term. The purpose of a Cash Budget is to predict when cash is going to be available, and when cash will be required. See Illustration III for a *Cash Budget: Projected* which can be used to anticipate cash needs and revenues. Illustration V shows a *Budget Report* which is dated and shows current figures, and the anticipated differences between the original estimates and these revised estimates.

Arts organizations have a generally bad reputation with businesses. Innumerable arts organizations default, procrastinate and don't pay their bills when they are due. It is not uncommon for organizations to be reduced to paying for every purchase with cash—a very inconvenient position to be in. It is desirable to do everything that you can to avoid putting yourself in this position. Try to pay your bills when they are due. If it is impossible, notify your creditors that your payment will be delayed, but that you will pay by a specific date. If you make a promise of this sort, though, it is essential that you keep it and meet this second deadline. Word of mouth—particularly badmouth—travels far.

There is, however, one way to turn this troublesome situation of a cash shortage around: When you anticipate a cash shortage, and know, for example, that you have been awarded a $5,000 grant from the National Endowment for the Arts, this may be the time to establish a line of credit at your bank, using your grant notification as collateral. Talk to an officer of the bank or savings institution who can appreciate the secondary benefits that might accrue to his/her institution from having you as a customer. Community involvement, helping the arts, developing good public relations material, may motivate your bank. Take out a small loan which will cover your expenses. Be sure to repay this loan when it comes due. Don't create any administrative problems for the bank. And remember, it is easier to borrow money when you aren't desperate.

One further budgeting tool is to do a *cost analysis* of a particular program or production or event over time to determine its profitability. A theatre company, for example, might want to decide how long to run a show, and could use this kind of analysis to determine what their break-even point is, or how long a show could be run profitably. Let's assume that the pre-production costs for *Hamlet* are $25,000. This will be a *fixed cost*; whether the show runs for one performance or a thousand, this figure will not change. After the show opens, it will cost $5,000 a week to run the show. A projection of audience attendance indicated that the play can generate $10,000 in revenues for the first two weeks, $8,000 for the second two weeks, $7,000 for the next four weeks, and $4,000 per week thereafter. Diagramming this reveals the following progression:

Week I	$30,000	$10,000	($20,000)
Week II	$35,000	$20,000	($15,000)
Week III	$40,000	$28,000	($12,000)
Week IV	$45,000	$36,000	($9,000)
Week V	$50,000	$43,000	($7,000)
Week VI	$55,000	$50,000	($5,000)
Week VII	$60,000	$57,000	($3,000)
Week VIII	$65,000	$64,000	($1,000)
Week IX	$70,000	$71,000	$1,000
Week X	$75,000	$75,000	-0-

This analysis would indicate that at the end of Week IX *Hamlet* would be in the black with a profit of $1,000. Thereafter, the show would be losing $1,000 per week. Ignoring other considerations, it would appear that a nine week run would be desirable. Should any of the fixed costs become variables—say the rental of the theatre were to be reduced by $1,500 per week after the ninth week—you would have to alter the chart to determine at what point it would then be desirable to end the run.

To summarize, try to keep the following general points in mind when you do your budgets:

1. Centralize the budgeting process. Have one person in charge who will know the ins and outs of the budget.

2. Make sure that there is a broad information base: that is, make sure that you get your facts from informed sources. Your shop manager may be the one person who knows that your $5,000 lathe is going to have to be replaced next year, but he will only indicate this if asked.

3. Don't take any of your programs for granted. Figure out what the costs are and what the returns are. Many organizations have small and insignificant programs which require a great deal of attention, or have small energy leaks which aren't significant in themselves, but taken as a whole result in a great waste of resources.

4. Make sure you know where and how people are spending time. You may not want your producer handling subscriptions over the phone, or spending a disproportionate amount of time doing the payroll. See that these investments of time are appropriate.

5. Make long range plans for the organization on a regular basis. Figure out where you want to go, and how to get there. Decide for the long haul, which revenue sources are going to be the most important. You may, for example, feel that foundation or corporate funds are going to be an important source of revenue three years from now if you are willing to make the investment of time and energy now. You could decide that your children's art education program, which is marginal now, will be lucrative in five years. Everything changes, so try to get into the habit of projecting into the future so that you can attempt to anticipate these changes.

6. Remember to check your current expenses and revenues against your budget throughout the course of the year. The budget is a yardstick which should indicate the extent to which you are fulfilling your goals.

7. Allow some funds in your budget for emergencies or miscellaneous expenses. Past experience should give you some indication of what this figure should be, whether it is 2% or 5%. If this figure is too high, and you have chronic shortages as a result of unexpected expenses, there is probably too little foresight in your budget planning.

Protecting Resources and Assets
It may seem self-evident that it is important to secure such things as cash and the corporate records, but often it is at this level that insurmountable difficulties originate. Getting down to basics, there should be adequate space to maintain a filing system, copies of unpaid bills, current corres-pondence—the day-to-day paperwork of the organization. It is important also to make sure that the corporate records are secure. Items that cannot be replaced, such as bank books, the corporate minutes, the charter, your IRS tax exemption, should be stored in a fireproof file, safe, or safety deposit box. Other records which give a detailed history of the finances of the corporation should also be stored in a secure, fireproof place. It is desirable that someone—your attorney or registered agent—keep xerox copies of all of these per-manent documents. For small and impecunious arts organ-izations, you might think of storing your records in an old refrigerator, which will provide some protection against fires, floods and other natural disasters.

The following check list includes most of the documents that you will want to secure:

1. Cancelled checks, deposit clips, bank statements.

2. Paid bills.

3. Charter

4. Insurance policies.

5. Operating budgets.

6. Reports to governmental agencies: IRS, state, or local.

7. Unemployment compensation reports.

8. Corporate minutes.

9. Board of directors.

10. Payroll book and tax deposits.

11. Loan agreements.

12. List of donors.

13. Mailing list.

14. Securities, savings account books, certificates of deposit.

Other resources which it is important to keep track of are the physical properties owned by the corporation. Typewriters, stage lights, sound equipment, sets, costumes, should be inventoried on a regular basis. Records should be kept which indicate the source of the item, the date purchased, cost, and serial number. Any items which are particularly valuable—a dimmer board for example—should be recorded with all of the above information and a copy of the original invoice.

A minor headache in most organizations are records relating to cash. Even organizations that don't have a significant currency flow must still deal with a petty cash account which must be balanced on a regular basis. It is customary to assign a small sum to a petty cash fund—say $100. When this amount is disbursed, the account is balanced with receipts provided for all expenditures, or in their absence a petty cash slip which indicates that so and so spent such and such an amount for this or that, plus the date. If $89 has been spent from the fund, a check for that amount is issued to the fund to bring the total back up to $100. It is desirable to have someone other than the person who disburses the money reconcile the account when new funds are added to the account.

For theatres and performing arts groups where there is a large amount of cash floating around, it is essential to have an efficient system for handling cash, tickets, change, and deposits. When there is a group involved in handling subscriptions and a large box office staff, I would recommend getting hold of a copy of an excellent booklet prepared by FEDAPT on *Box Office Guidelines.* (FEDAPT, Foundation for the Extension and Development of the American Professional Theatre, 1500 Broadway, N.Y., N.Y. 10036, (212) 869-9690. The booklet is $5.75 postage paid.) For organizations whose needs may not be quite so complex, I have included a *Box Office Report,* Illustration VI, which can be used to keep track of box office receipts. When you set up your box office system, keep the following points in mind:

1. Select reliable people to handle your box office funds. You may want to get them bonded, which will insure you against any loss should your box office personnel turn out to be thieves. Insurance or bonding companies handle this type of insurance.

2. Have separate change funds for each cashier.

3. Reconcile each change fund after every performance.

4. If possible use preprinted tickets with the date, performance, and price printed on each ticket. Have a detachable stub on each ticket which can be used to reconcile attendance with the cash receipts.

5. Reconcile ticket stubs with box office receipts after each performance.

6. Deposit all cash in the bank as soon as possible.

The other major source of cash will be the funds in the checking and saving accounts. These funds are less vulnerable than currency which is sitting around your office, but must still be protected. Here are some things to consider when you set up your system for handling your checking and savings accounts.

1. Consider requiring two signatures on checks and withdrawals from the savings account. This system may create more problems than it is worth because it will necessitate the presence of two authorized employees any time that it is necessary to write a check.

2. Limit the number of people with authority to write checks.

3. Someone other than the individuals who write the checks should monitor the account and reconcile the bank statements.

4. Require a reconciliation of the account at the end of the month.

5. Consider bonding employees who handle checks or cash.

6. Clearly specify who and what amounts can be paid out by any individual at their own discretion.

In most organizations these financial functions and decisions are determined at different levels. The board of directors is responsible for setting the overall financial policy and approving budgets, and is ultimately liable for the financial actions of the corporation. The managing or executive director is responsible for seeing that the directives of the board are carried out by the staff, and within the guidelines set by the board, responsible for making the day-to-day financial decisions. The staff is then assigned the function of disbursing cash, submitting budget information, keeping records, etc. The accountant sets the policies regarding how the records are kept, what kind of documentation is required for each transaction, and which procedures are to be followed. The bookkeeper assembles this information and records it in the various journals and ledgers set up by the accountant. Finally, an outside auditor may be called in to verify that the system designed by the accountant is adequate and that the information is being properly handled by the bookkeeper. In smaller organizations many of these functions will be assumed by the same person.

Bookkeeping

"*Accounting* is the system for collecting, summarizing, and reporting financial information. *Bookkeeping* refers to the process of recording financial information within the structure of the accounting system." These definitions made by Mary Wehle are useful for distinguishing the two related and at times overlapping activities. The two together create a system which makes it possible for you to understand your current economic situation and to project for future needs.

The basic financial instrument for a small arts organization is the checkbook. Most of the information relating to receipts of funds and disbursements can be obtained from the deposit slips and the check stubs that are retained in the checkbook. If you are just starting, or are dissatisfied with your current bank, you should establish a checking account in a bank that will be likely to service your current and future financial needs. You should look for a bank that is sympathetic to the arts, and willing to go out on a limb for "worthwhile" activities. You should also look for a bank which will give you free checking because of your not-for-profit status.

In actually selecting a checking system, look through all of the possibilities, and select the system that fills your needs. For organizations with a limited number of employees— under fifteen—I recommend a system which makes it possible to write payroll checks and general checks from the same account. In this system, there is a detachable stub for the employees payroll record, and space in the checkbook stub for the same withholding information.

If you are in a position to, you might think of buying a computerized bookkeeping system right from the start.

They require a checkbook with a carbon record of each transaction. The carbon copies are sent to the service at the end of the month. The cost of these services varies, depending on the number of transactions each month, plus a figure for setting up the system. These services are probably too sophisticated and costly for very small organizations, but for larger organizations they provide a simple way of getting detailed financial information very quickly. Usually included in the service is preparation of your monthly or quarterly statements for the IRS, the state, and FICA.

No matter which system you choose and what kind of account you set up, you will usually have to present the bank with your articles of incorporation, a list of officers, and a list of board members. You will also have to decide who can write checks, and how many signatures are required for each check. Though it affords some additional security, from my experience it is awkward to require two signatures on each check. It is advisable, though, to limit the number of people authorized to issue checks.

With respect to writing checks, make sure that the check stub accurately records to whom the check was written, the date, the amount, and what the payment was for. It is useful to include a precise description of the item—"flyers for Installation Show"—and then the account to which the item should be charged—"printing" or "account #471." For each check that is written there should be supporting documentation which can include an invoice, petty cash slip, or note. On this document indicate the check number, the date payment was made, and the person who wrote the check. I have found that a good way of dealing with these invoices is to purchase an alphabetized, expanding cardboard file ($6 or $7) and to file invoices alphabetically and by date. At the end of the year the folder can simply be stored with the records for that financial year, and a new file purchased.

For receipts and deposits I recommend having two systems. The first system will be a "Cash Receipt Book" which should have at least one original and one copy for each receipt. (Illustration VII) In this book you can record individual receipts of income: tuition, donations, sales of books, performance income, grants, etc. In addition to providing you with supporting documentation for your deposits, this book can provide you with information for your donors list and student mailing list as well as receipts for your clients. It is possible that you will only want to record individual sales in this book, excluding performance income, grants, etc.

The deposit slips in your checkbook will record the actual deposits to the bank, and will be the basis for additional record keeping. On these stubs you should indicate the date, the account to which this money is being deposited, e.g., "tuition" or "7359", and the source of the funds, e.g., "$50 from Jay Pearl." Try not to make deposits to more than one account on each deposit slip. This will complicate your handling of the information when the transaction is recorded in your journal.

At the end of the month you will receive a statement from your bank. Reconcile your figures with the bank's as soon as possible. There are a number of common problems which sometimes make it difficult to reconcile the two. First there are bank charges—either a monthly charge for your account, or charges for special services like stopping a check or for printing new checks and deposit slips. Be sure to record these charges in your checkbook. Second, outstanding checks may have to be carried forward from previous months, and may remain uncashed for the entire year. These should be carried through the year, then cancelled, and rewritten if necessary. Finally, there will be deposits which you have made which will have been returned to you because the checks bounced. These checks must either be destroyed or redeposited. In either case you will have to account for a double deposit, offset by a single bank charge in the amount of the check, or a deposit offset by a bank charge of the same amount.

Once you have reconciled your bank statement and your checking account, you can proceed to the next step, which will be to summarize all of this financial information in a *Journal* or *Book of Original Entry*. We begin with a *Cash*

Receipts Journal, Illustration VIII. This journal includes the period which is being summarized—in this case the month of January, 1978, the source of the funds, and the date of deposit in the bank, the account in which they were deposited, and the income account to which they are to be attributed. In the Journal we encounter for the first time double-entry bookkeeping. You will note that in this Journal there is a summary of the account in which the funds were deposited on the left hand side—the *debit* side, and a corresponding breakdown of the deposits in terms of the accounts to which the deposits are to be *credited.* The two halves of the system should total the same amount—because the same funds are being accounted for on each side. What we have done is to create a mathematical check on the accuracy of our system. In accounting, debit and credit have different meanings than in real life, and are used to indicate that in the case of a debit, an amount has been entered in the left column, and with a credit that an amount has been entered in the right column. The two are sometimes abbreviated *dr* for debit and *cr* for credit.

On the credit side of the Journal we have set up accounts which indicate the origin of the funds that have been deposited. For small organizations there may be just a few sources of income. For larger organizations the sources of funds may number in the hundreds, in which case it would make things easier to assign code numbers to them. One further detail: when you transfer information from the checkbook to the Journal, a process known as *posting,* you should indicate in the checkbook that the transaction has been recorded in the Journal. Our second journal is the *Cash Disbursement Journal,* which categorizes and summarizes the money that has been paid out during the course of the month—Illustration IX. This information is gathered from the check stubs in the checkbook. This journal is set up in such a way that it indicates the period for which the Journal is kept, in this case the month of January, 1978, the person or company to whom the payment is made, the date, the check number, the amount, and the account to which the transaction is to be charged. In this case we are assuming that there is no separate Payroll Account, so that in item five, the amount of John Smith's payroll check plus the amount deducted for federal and state withholding taxes appears on one side of the journal page, while on the other the gross salary or total "payroll" figure is recorded. The same double-entry system is used here as in the Cash Receipts Journal. Similarly, all of the accounts could be coded so that instead of the titles of the accounts we could simply have a numerical description of the account. With this Journal also, the two halves must balance, indicating that it is at least mathematically accurate.

Two other Journals which supplement the Cash Receipts Journal and the Cash Disbursement Journal are the *General Journal* and the *Payroll Journal*. The General Journal—Illustration X—is set up to deal with mistakes from previous months, and to record transactions that have not resulted from cash receipts or disbursements, such as payment made by board members for goods or services. Finally, this Journal can be used to record taxes that have been withheld, and their subsequent payment into separate tax accounts. Note that in this case the taxes for the quarter were held and deposited in toto at the conclusion of the quarter.

Payroll records are generally summarized in a separate journal which facilitates filing the monthly, quarterly, and year-end reports with the government. These record books are readily available at stationery stores. See Illustration XI for a sample. In addition, the IRS publishes and distributes a complete payroll packet which includes all of the forms that you will require, tables of deductions, and a calendar indicating when forms which employers must file are due. The same information should be available from your state. You will probably have an employer identification number which you received when you filed your application for an IRS tax exemption. If not, you must acquire one in order to report all of your payroll information.

Non-profit organizations can apply for an exemption from social security payments. If your organization is flush, you should elect to make these payments for the benefit of your employees. Many organizations for the sake of economy choose not to. Unemployment compensation poses a more complicated problem. Arts organizations have historically used unemployment insurance as a way to finance their activities; it is not inappropriate to think of unemployment compensation as a form of middle-class welfare in this case. Arts organizations frequently employ personnel for part of the year and then have them apply for unemployment compensation for the rest of the year. Though your unemployment compensation rate will go up—currently the range is from 2.7% of total wages to 3.5%, if you have a poor record for unemployment claims—it is a lucrative option, should you choose it.

The Journals, or Books of Original Entry, constitute the first part of a bookkeeping system. When they have been completed, this information is summarized once more in *Ledgers, Books of Secondary Entry*. In the Ledger each account that appears in the journals—"tuition", "grants", "utilities", "rent"—is totalled on a separate page or in a separate column. In this fashion it is possible to see how much income has been generated by any given activity, and how much cash has been disbursed for any function— Illustration XII.

If your organization is small, and there are a limited number of categories for income and expenses, you can simply label each account in your journals and in your ledger. In larger organizations this becomes cumbersome, and it is common to set up a *Chart of Accounts,* which provides an account number for each item, and a guide on how to handle problematic or discretionary items. In setting up your Chart of Accounts you should select those items which apply to your organization, and use the accounts that you might need that aren't listed by selecting an unused number in the proper account category. You should of course make up your own list and include a description of your whole bookkeeping procedure in this separate handbook. Your Chart of Accounts, in addition to providing a listing of accounts and account numbers, is also a guide book to your particular bookkeeping system.

Additional reports such as a Trial Balance, Balance Sheet, and Income Statement can then be taken from the Ledger.

Financial Policy

Before you set up your accounting system there are a number of questions of financial policy which you must decide. The most basic question is whether to use a *cash* or an *accrual* accounting system. To explain the difference between the two as simply as possible, a cash system records income when cash is received, and expenditures when cash is paid out. An accrual method records income when it is *earned*, and expenditures when goods or services are *used*. In an accrual system it is not important when a bill is sent or cash received, but when the activity takes place. An accrual system remedies one significant problem with cash accounting, which is that with a cash system it is possible to incur large unrecorded debts which don't appear in any financial reports until the bill is actually received or payment made. Poorly run organizations can find themselves in awful, and unexpected, financial shape as a result. The other side of the coin is that an organization could have substantial grants which were promised but not received during an accounting period which would bias the financial reports in the other direction. Or a group could receive a three-year grant with payment made in the first year. In a cash system the total amount would be recorded as income in the first year, and none of it would appear as income in financial reports for the second and third years. The problem with the accrual system, however, is that it requires considerably more time and energy.

I recommend that small- and medium-size arts organizations use a *modified* accrual system. In this system critical adjustments of large sums can be included in the financial reporting. A report of this sort appears as Illustration XVIII.

A second area which poses financial problems has to do with recording income that comes in the form of donated services. Historically arts organizations have relied heavily on these. To give a true picture of the operation of the organization, these donations should be recorded. The question is where to draw the lines. For example, should the chairman of the board—a fancy corporate attorney—be considered to have donated services, and if so in what amount? When an accountant donates his services to the organization in order to prepare financial statements, how should his donated services be accounted for? What of the time put into mailings and clean-up and answering the phone by volunteers? The guidelines are unclear for these questions, but a rule of thumb which you could use, is to include donations, and assign a dollar amount to, services which are rendered that *would be paid for,* under normal circumstances. Hence, if you would do the mailing yourself in the absence of volunteers, and if you would only consider an unpaid chairman of the board, you should not include these as donated services in financial reports. If on the other hand you're willing to pay an accountant for preparing your financial statements, but you get someone to donate his or her services, you should count this as a donation.

A third question for arts organizations is the capitalization of assets. The materials of the arts are distinctive in that they have value, in large part, only to the organization that is using them, or perhaps to a few similar organizations. Scores, plays, scenery, costumes may only have value to your group. If you were to fold this year, they might be unsalable. Even though you may use costumes for several years, it is conservative and desirable to expense them in their entirety for the years in which they are purchased. On the other hand, a stereo sound system, which could be disposed of readily, should be capitalized in the normal way. It is best to be conservative, and to allow for all of the uncertainties that exist in the art world.

Nonprofit organizations have one problem to deal with that relates to gifts or grants to the institution which are allocated for specific purposes. To account for these gifts, *funds* are established by the organization so that donors can receive financial reports on the disposition of their gifts. Of course some gifts will simply be given to the organization with no strings attached. These unrestricted funds pose no accounting problems. Restricted gifts must, for accounting purposes, be dealt with as isolated entities with their own assets, liabilities, and funds which must balance. These *funds* will be self-balancing microcosms within the larger world of your accounting system. There are a considerable number of different kinds of funds that your organization might have to account for—Endowment Funds, Annuity and Life Income Funds, Plant Funds, Agency Funds—all of which must be dealt with differently.

In the final analysis it is worthwhile to keep in mind that accounting by its very nature is conservative and under-stated, and that members of the profession tend to conform to those same biases. Arts organizations usually come into existence through leaps of faith and are sustained by acts of will. Most sound financial advice would argue against starting in the first place, and caution against most expansion thereafter. Though accountants and financial managers are useful, think of these professionals as "hired guns"— go to them when you want a job done. As one business mogul I know puts it, "Good accountants are great at saving money, but I never met one who knew how to make it."

Single Entry Bookkeeping

Double entry bookkeeping is accomplished by simultaneous entries to "real" accounts (assets and liabilities) and "nominal" accounts (income and expense). This system provides a mathematical check on the accuracy of transaction posting and is the system that should be followed by most organizations.

Single entry bookkeeping emphasizes the recording of income and expenses by the recording of cash receipts and disbursements. While this system does not provide a self balancing bookkeeping system, it is possible to provide for mathematical accuracy by building certain checks and proofs into the system.

The small organization which does not have a full-time bookkeeper, accountant or financial manager, might consider using the single entry system because it is much simpler to use for untrained, part-time personnel and it may provide enough financial information to satisfy the needs of the organization. Furthermore, if the organization maintains its accounting records by the single entry, cash method throughout the year, it might consider engaging a professional accountant to "close" the year by converting to an accrual basis from which financial statements can be prepared.

To use the single entry system, the following records have to be prepared:

Cash Receipts Journal—Exhibit 1
Cash Receipts Summary—Exhibit 2
Check Disbursements Journal—Exhibit 3
Check Disbursements Summary—Exhibit 4
Proof of Cash Transactions—Exhibit 5 and
End of the Year Bank Reconciliation.
(Cash transactions should be proved and reconciled on a monthly basis, as well.)

From the data collected in these records a worksheet is prepared to collect and further summarize the transactions (Exhibit 6). This worksheet may be used to prepare cash basis financial statements (Exhibit 7) or it may be used as a starting point to prepare a cash to accrual basis worksheet (Exhibit 8) from which accrual basis financial statements can be prepared (Exhibit 9).

Illustration I

Program Budget: Expenditures, Peacock Players 6-1-77 to 5-31-78

Expenditures	Primary activities				Support activities			
	main stage (1)	show-case (2)	school (3)	(4)	administrative (5)	subscription (6)	general (7)	totals (8)
1 salaries	$14,000—	4,000—	10,000—		6,000—	4,000—	2,000—	40,000—
2 office supplies	200—	50—	300—		500—	200—	200—	1,450—
3 utilities	1,100—	300—	1,400—		1,000—	200—	400—	4,400—
4 promotion	2,000—	50—	700—		50—	1,000—	300—	4,100—
5 insurance	1,000—	500—	200—		50—	50—	50—	1,850—
6 rent	600—	200—	600—		100—	100—	200—	1,800—
7								
8 totals	18,900—	5,100—	13,200—		7,700—	5,550—	3,350—	53,600—
9								

Illustration II

Program Budget: Revenue, Peacock Players 6-1-77 to 5-31-78

Income	general funds (1)	main stage (2)	show-case (3)	school (4)	totals (5)	6	7	8
1 subscriptions		18,000—			18,000—			
2 ticket sales		6,000—	4,000—		10,000—			
3 tuition				6,000—	6,000—			
4 foundation grants	1,000—	2,000—	1,000—		4,000—			
5 government grants	6,000—	2,000—	1,000—		9,000—			
6 contributions	1,000—				1,000—			
7								
8 totals	8,000—	28,000—	6,000—	6,000—	48,000—			
9								

Illustration III

Cash Budget Projected – 1st Quarter 1978

	1	2	3	4
Opening Balance	January 16,000 –	February 15,600 –	March 14,800 –	
Income				
subscriptions	2000 –	1,000 –	1,000 –	
ticket sales	500 –	500 –	500 –	
foundation grants	1,000 –			
government grants		2000 –		
contributions	500 –			
Total income	4,000 –	3500 –	1,500 –	
Expenses				
salaries	2100 –	2000 –	2500 –	
office supplies	100 –	100 –	200 –	
utilities	200 –	300 –	400 –	
promotion	200 –	100 –	500 –	
insurance			500 –	
rent	1800 –	1800 –	1800 –	
Total Expenses	4400 –	4300 –	5900 –	
Closing Balance	15,600 –	14,800 –	10,400 –	

Illustration IV

Cash Report January 31, 1978

Accounts	1 opening balance	2 add deposits	3 subtract withdrawals	4 closing balance
Continental Bank checking acc't	6000 –	4000 –	4400 –	5600 –
Aetna Bank savings account	5000 –	Ø	Ø	5000 –
totals	11,000 –	4000 –	4400 –	* 10,600 –
Short Term Investments				
certificate of deposit due 2-28-78	5000 –	Ø	Ø	5000 –
totals	5000 –	Ø	Ø	* 5000 –
total cash 1-31-78				15,600 –

Illustration V

BUDGET REPORT March 31, 1978	Annual Budget	Actual March 31	Projected to Dec. 31	Favorable (unfavorable) difference	
Income					1
					2
Subscriptions	18,000—	4,000—	19,000—	(1,000-)	3
Ticket Sales	10,000—	1,500—	10,000—	1,500—	4
Foundation Grants	4,000—	1,000-	2,000-	(1,000-)	5
Gov't Grants	9,000—	2,000—	5,000—	(2,000)	6
Contributions	1,000-	500-	500-	0	7
					8
Total Income	42,000—	9,000—	30,500-	(2,500-)	9
					10
Expenses					11
					12
Salaries	30,000-	6,600-	24,000—	600—	13
Office Supplies	1,150-	400-	400-	(350-)	14
Utilities	3,000-	900-	2,200-	100-	15
Promotion	3,400-	800-	2,000-	(600-)	16
Insurance	1,650-	500-	900-	(250-)	17
Rent	1,800-	5,400-	0	3,600—	18
					19
Total Expenses	41,000-	14,600—	29,500-	3,100—	20
					21
					22
less expenses	1,000—	(5,600-)	1,000-	(5,600-)	23

Illustration VI

Box Office Report – Performance "Trance Dance" January 16, 1978			
COIN			
Denomination	Total		Amount
$ .01	300		$ 3.00
.05	50		2.50
.10	60		6.00
.25	40		10.00
.50	40		20.00
1.00	1		1.00
TOTAL			42.50
CURRENCY			
Denomination	Total		Amount
$1	86		86.00
5	20		100.00
20	40		800.00
50	10		500.00
100	6		600.00
Total			2,086.00
Total Cash			2,128.50
Original Amount (minus)			100.00
Box Office Sales			2,028.50

Illustration VII

RECEIPT No 5021
Date 1/16 1978
Received From Richard Todd
Address 210 W. 108th St NY
NY 10015   787-4370   Dollars $90
For Tuition - Ballet I
By TH

ACCOUNT		HOW PAID	
AMT OF ACCOUNT	90	CASH	
AMT PAID	90	CHECK	90
BALANCE DUE	-0-	MONEY ORDER	

RECEIPT No 5022
Date 1/17 1978
Received From Hortense Walton
Address 806 W. Diversey Chicago
60614   472-0710   Dollars $50
For Unrestricted Donation
By TH

ACCOUNT		HOW PAID	
AMT OF ACCOUNT	50	CASH	50
AMT PAID	50	CHECK	
BALANCE DUE	-0-	MONEY ORDER	

RECEIPT No 5023
Date 1/18 1978
Received From Box Office (Theatre)
Address "Ashes"
Dollars $1065
For Performance Income
By TH

ACCOUNT		HOW PAID	
AMT OF ACCOUNT	1065	CASH	1000
AMT PAID	1065	CHECK	65
BALANCE DUE	65	MONEY ORDER	

RECEIPT No 5024
Date 1/18 1978
Received From National Endowment for the Arts
Address Washington, D.C.
Dollars $300
For "Dance in the Schools" Grant
Summer - 1978
By TH

ACCOUNT		HOW PAID	
AMT OF ACCOUNT	300	CASH	
AMT PAID	300	CHECK	300
BALANCE DUE	-0-	MONEY ORDER	

Illustration VIII

CASH RECEIPTS JOURNAL   January 1978

		DEBIT		CREDIT					
Source	date	checking amount 1	savings amount 2	subscriptions 3	ticket sales 4	contributions 5	foundations 6	Gov't 7	miscellaneous 8
Subscriptions	15	200		200					
ticket sales	8	150			150				
ticket sales	9	220			220				
Paul Smith	14	500				500			
Lilly Foundation	16	2000					2000		
NEA	21		1500					1500	
Peoples Gas (refund)	26	70							70
Total		3140	1500	200	370	500	2000	1500	70
		4640							4640

Illustration IX

Cash Disbursements Journal   January 1978

* No separate account for payroll. Taxes withheld and payments to Federal & State gov't are noted in the General Journal.

		1	2	3	4	5	6	7	8	9	10	11
Payee	date	check #	amount	Federal tax	State tax	promotion	production	office	utilities	payroll	General account	amount
1 OK office Supply	13	101	46 -					46 -				
2 Edison Co.	7	102	114 -						114 -			
3 Daily News	9	103	75 -			75 -						
4 AA Lumber	12	104	106 -				106 -					
5 John Smith *	15	105	500 -	150 -	50 -					700 -		
6 City of Chicago	18	106	110 -								theatre license	110 -
7 Philip Orro Inc	23	107	80 -			80 -						
8 State of Illinois	28	108	50 -								state tax	50 -
9												
10 Totals			1081 -	150 -	50 -	155 -	106 -	46 -	114 -	700 -		160 -
11			1081 -									1081 -
12												
13												

Illustration X

General Journal

			1	2	3	4
date	Account		amount	date	check #	amount
1 Jan	Federal W/H Tax		150 -			
2 Feb	"		40 -			
3 Mar	"		150 -			
4						
5	totals		340 -	4/30	183	340 -
6						
7						
8						

Illustration XI

WEEK ENDING January 31, 1978

	M/S	Category	HOURS							RATE	EARNINGS				DEDUCTIONS				NET PAY		CUMULATIVE TOTALS			
NAME			TOTAL HOURS	REGULAR	OVERTIME	OTHER	TOTAL WAGES	SOC. SEC.	U.S. WITH TAX	STATE WITH TAX											SOC. SEC.	U.S. WITH TAX	STATE WITH TAX	
Paul Maguire	M 3		8 8 8 8 3		78			78		4 56	3 50	50		69 44	312		15 24	14 00	2 00			
Carol Wright	S 1		43	2 20	88	9 90		97 90	5 73	12 90	1 85		78 02	341 60	22 92	49 20	7 40					
David Lerner	M 4			120 1		9 1		129 1	7 55	8 90	1 35		111 20	516 1	30 20	35 60	5 40					
TOTALS				286 1	9 90	9 1		304 90	17 84	24 90	3 60		258 66	1219 60	71 36	98 80	14 80					

Form by permission from Dome Improved Payroll Book,
Dome Enterprises, Inc., Providence, R.I. ©1974.

Illustration XII

Ledger 1978

Promotion #512

Source	date	amount
Cash Disbursements Jl CD-1	1/8	22 1
"	12	46 1
"	14	33 1
" CD-4	2/6	112 1
" CD-5	15	69 1
" CD-6	3/1	56 1

Checking Account #101

Source	date	debits	credits	balance
	1/31			10,500 —
Cash Disbursements Journal CD-5	2/28		51 00 —	
Cash Receipts Journal CR-4	28	5000 —		
	28			10,400 —

Illustration XIII

INCOME & EXPENSES: CASH, ACCRUAL, & MODIFIED ACCRUAL

December 31, 1977 (end of year)

	CASH	ACCRUAL ADJUSTMENT	ACCRUAL
Income			
subscriptions	17,000—	-1,000— ①	16,000—
ticket sales	14,000—		14,000—
foundation grants	4,000—	-2,000— ②	2,000—
gov't grants	8,000—		8,000—
contributions	2,000—		2,000—
Total Income	45,000—	3,000—	42,000—
Expenses			
salaries	30,000—		30,000—
office supplies	1,000—		1,000—
utilities	3,000—		3,000—
promotion	3,500—	-1,000— ③	2,500—
insurance	1,500—	-500— ④	1,000—
rent	1,500—		1,500—
Total Expense	40,500—	1,500—	39,000—

① $1000 in subscriptions for 1978 season
② $2,000 of grant allocated for program in 1978
③ $1,000 in brochures printed for summer of 1978
④ $500 prepayment of liability insurance for 1978 and 1979

CASH RECEIPTS JOURNAL

1979 Date	Description	Cash Received	Bank Deposit	Dues	Contri-bution	Grants	Special Events Proj. 1	Proj. 2	Proj. 3
Jan. 5	Grant—QMB Organization	$100						$100	
Jan. 5	Grant—Jackson Foundation	80	$180			$80			
Jan. 14	Dues Joe Boyoka	20	20	20					
Jan. 29	Gift Nancy Pick	50			$50				
Jan. 30	Receipts from Performance	550	600					550	
	Total	$800	$800	$20	$50	$80		$650	

Exhibit 1

CASH RECEIPTS SUMMARY

1979	Cash Received	Dues	Contri-bution	Grants	Special Events Proj. 1	Proj. 2	Proj. 3
January	$800	$ 20	$50	$ 80		$650	
February	400	—	10	360	$30		
March	300	200	20		80		
Total	$20,000	$3,000	$3,000	$5,000	$6,000	$1,000	$2,000

Exhibit 2

CASH DISBURSEMENTS JOURNAL

Date	Payee	Check No.	Amount of Check	General Expenses			Special Events		
				Office	Salaries	Misc.	Proj. 1	Proj. 2	Proj. 3
Jan. 4	Smith	101	$100	$100					
Jan. 6	Jones	102	60		$60				
Jan. 12	Whatever	103	200				Adv. $200		
Jan. 16	None	104	200				Printing 200		
Jan. 18	Example	105	40				Adv. 40		
Jan. 21	Com-Edison	106	80			$80			
Jan. 22	Brown	107	100				Salary 100		
Totals			$2050	$250	$100	$200	$1,500		
Details				Utilities		$80	Printing $ 200		
				Telephone		100	Adv. 240		
				Postage		20	Salary 560		
							Postage 100		
							Misc. 400		
						$200	$1,500		

Exhibit 3

CASH DISBURSEMENTS—SUMMARY

		General Expenses					Special Events Project 1			
	Total	Office	Salaries	Utilities	Telephone	Postage	Other	Adv.	Print.	Salary	Other
Jan.	$1,900	$100	$100	$ 80	$100	$20	$—	$240	$200	$560	$500
Feb.	2,000	200	700	10	90	10	—	200	100	400	200
Mar.	1,600	200	300	50	50	—	100	100	300	200	300
Totals	$18,000	$2,000	$5,000	$600	$400	$100	$200	$1,000	$2,000	$3,000	$3,700

Exhibit 4

SIMPLIFIED SINGLE ENTRY SYSTEM
PROOF OF CASH TRANSACTIONS

Cash in bank—beginning of year	$ 4,000
Cash receipts per summary	20,000
Total	24,000
Cash disbursed per summary	22,000
Cash in bank—end of year	$ 2,000

BANK RECONCILIATION

Ending cash balance per bank	$ 4,400
Deposits in transit	
(received by bank January 4, 1980)	1,000
Total	5,400

Checks outstanding

Check No.	Amount	
184	$1,200	
190	600	
194	600	
197	1,000	
Total		3,400

Ending cash in bank as reconciled	$ 2,000

EXHIBIT 5

SUMMARY OF CASH TRANSACTIONS
YEAR ENDED DECEMBER 31, 19___

Summary of Cash Transactions

Accounts	Receipts (Exhibit 2)	Disbursements (Exhibit 4)
Income tax withheld		$ (500)
Dues	$10,000	
CAPA grants	5,000	
Director salary		5,000
Payroll taxes		1,000
Insurance		1,000
Rent		2,000
Telephone		500
Etc.		8,000
Special Event No. 1		
Admissions	2,000	
Actors		1,000
Rent		1,000
Producer		500
Etc.		500
Special Event No. 2		
Grant	3,000	
Publisher		1,000
Totals	20,000	22,000
		20,000
Disbursements in excess of receipts		(2,000)
Cash balance—January 1, ___		4,000
Cash balance—December 31, ___		$ 2,000

Exhibit 6

STATEMENT OF ASSETS, LIABILITIES AND FUND BALANCE
(CASH METHOD OF ACCOUNTING)
DECEMBER 31, 19

ASSETS

CASH	$2,000

LIABILITIES

INCOME TAX WITHHELD	500
FUND BALANCE	$1,500

CASH RECEIPTS AND DISBURSEMENTS
YEAR ENDED DECEMBER 31, 19____

	special Event No. 1	Special Event No. 2	Total
Cash receipts	$2,000	$3,000	$5,000
Disbursements			
Salaries	1,000	—	1,000
Rent	1,000	—	1,000
Producer	500	—	500
Publisher	—	1,000	1,000
Other	500	—	500
	3,000	1,000	4,000
Project cash surplus/(deficit)	$(1,000)	$2,000	1,000
General operations		10,000	
Dues		5,000	
CAPA Grants		15,000	
Total receipts			
Disbursements			
Director salary	5,000		
Payroll taxes	1,000		
Insurance	1,000		
Rent	2,000		
Utilities	1,000		
Telephone	500		
Other	8,000		
Total disbursements		18,500	
Operations cash (deficit)			(3,500)
Disbursements in excess of cash receipts			(2,500)
Fund—balance (cash basis) beginning of year			4,000
Fund—balance (cash basis) end of year			$(1,500)

Exhibit 7

Accounts	Cash Basis Results (A) Receipts	Disbursements	Accrual Balance Beginning of Year	Reverse Beginning Accruals	
Cash	$20,000	$(22,000)	$ 4,000		
Dues receivable			9,000	(1)	$(9,000)
CAPA receivables			1,000	(2)	(1,000)
Prepaid insurance			1,000	(3)	(1,000)
Accounts payable			(3,000)	(4)	3,000
Accrued salaries			(2,000)	(5)	2,000
Payroll taxes				(6)	1,000
Income tax withheld		(500)			
Fund balance			(9,000)		
Dues	(10,000)			(1)	9,000
CAPA grants	(5,000)			(1)	1,000
Director salary		5,000		(5)	(2,000)
Payroll taxes		1,000		(6)	(1,000)
Insurance		1,000		(3)	1,000
Rent		2,000			
Utilities		1,000			
Telephone		500			
Etc.		8,000		(4)	(3,000)
Depreciation					
Special Event No. 1					
Admissions	(2,000)				
Actors		1,000			
Rent		1,000			
Producer		1,000			
Etc.		500			
		500			
Special Event No. 2					
Grant	(3,000)				
Publisher					
Advertising		1,000			
Mailings					

Exhibit 8

Record Ending Accruals	Accrual Basis Trial Balance	Balance Sheet	General	Revenues and Expenses Special Event No. 1	Special Event No. 2
	$ 2,000	$ 2,000			
1) $11,000	11,000	11,000			
2) 2,000	2,000	2,000			
4) (6,000)	(6,000)	(6,000)			
5) (3,000)	(3,000)	(3,000)			
6) (2,000)	(2,000)	(2,000)			
	(500)	(500)			
	(9,000)	(9,000)			
1) (11,000)	(12,000)		$(12,000)		
2) (2,000)	(6,000)		(6,000)		
5) 3,000	6,000		6,000		
6) 2,000	2,000		2,000		
	2,000		2,000		
	2,000		2,000		
	1,000		1,000		
	500		500		
4) 4,000	9,000		9,000		
	(2,000)			$(2,000)	
	1,000			1,000	
	1,000			1,000	
	500			500	
	500			500	
	(3,000)				$(3,000)
	1,000				1,000
4) 1,000	1,000				1,000
4) 1,000	1,000				1,000
—	—	$(5,500)	4,500	$ 1,000	—
		(B)	1,000		
			$ 5,500		
			(C)		

(A) From receipts and disbursements summaries
(B) Decrease in fund balance
(C) Expenses in excess of revenues

STATEMENT OF ASSETS, LIABILITIES AND FUND BALANCE
DECEMBER 31, 19__

ASSETS

CASH		$ 2,000
RECEIVABLES		
Dues	$11,000	
CAPA vouchers	2,000	13,000
TOTAL CURRENT ASSETS		$15,000

LIABILITIES AND FUND BALANCE

CURRENT LIABILITIES		
Accounts payable		$ 6,000
Accrued salary		3,000
Accrued payroll taxes		2,000
Employees' income taxes withheld		500
Total current liabilities		11,500
FUND BALANCE—beginning of year	$ 9,000	
Less—excess of expenses		
over revenues for the year	(5,500)	
Fund balance—end of year		3,500
TOTAL LIABILITIES AND FUND BALANCE		$15,000

Exhibit 9

STATEMENT OF REVENUES AND EXPENSES
YEAR ENDED DECEMBER 31, 19__

	Special Event No. 1	Special Event No. 2	Total
Revenue	$ 2,000	$ 3,000	$ 5,000
Expenses			
Salaries	1,500	1,000	2,500
Rent	1,000		1,000
Advertising		1,000	1,000
Other	500		500
Mailings		1,000	1,000
Total	3,000	3,000	6,000
Project surplus/(deficit)	$(1,000)	$ —	(1,000)
General operations			
Dues		$12,000	
CAPA grants		6,000	
Total revenue		18,000	
Expenses			
Director salary	$ 6,000		
Payroll taxes	2,000		
Insurance	2,000		
Rent	2,000		
Utilities	1,000		
Telephone	500		
Etc.	9,000		
Total		22,500	
General operations deficit			(4,500)
Excess of expenses over revenues			$(5,500)

Albert S. Kaplan, C.P.A.
Tem Horwitz

Exhibit 10

Setting Up & Maintaining Not-for-Profit, Tax Exempt Corporations

The not-for-profit method of doing business among cultural organizations has become increasingly popular as operational costs have risen and government, foundation and corporate support for the arts has grown. This chapter will outline some of the things one should consider when deciding whether to incorporate not-for-profit, the procedure by which a not-for-profit corporation is formed and tax exemption recognized, and the operational problems and features of not-for-profit, tax exempt organizations. Laws regulating not-for-profit corporations differ from state to state, so much of this text must necessarily be presented in terms of general rules which may or may not hold true in your own state. Reference will also be made to the law in Illinois when that will be helpful. Because differing laws require this generality, and because properly organizing a not-for-profit corporation to qualify for and then obtain tax exemption may be quite complex, the services of a skilled attorney will be needed for most beginning organizations. Familiarizing oneself with the information in this chapter will nevertheless be beneficial, for the better prepared and more knowledgeable a group is about the processes they are setting in motion, the better professionals will be able to serve them.

It is important to keep the distinction between not-for-profit and tax-exempt in mind throughout this chapter. Not-for-profit refers to the legal structure which an organization adopts under the not-for-profit laws of the state. This not-for-profit corporation then applies to various taxing authorities for an exemption from the tax which the authority is attempting to impose. Although it is necessary to be not-for-profit to be recognized as tax exempt, not-for-profit status does not guarantee tax exemption. And exemption from one tax, such as income tax, will not grant an exemption from other taxes such as sales or property taxes. Although not-for-profit and tax-exempt status are important legal distinctions, most not-for-profit corporations contemplate a subsequent application for tax exemption. Therefore this chapter will speak separately of the two concepts, but they must necessarily intertwine.

Why Not-for-Profit?

While many cultural organizations operate on a not-for-profit basis today, the decision to go the not-for-profit route should not be an automatic one. What are the considerations one should take into account when deciding which method of organization is most appropriate?

One should first ask the question: Is this enterprise being entered into solely as a vehicle for my own individual talents or the talents of a few, or is the benefit of the operation intended to be more broadly based? Is this venture intended to advance and promote a specific work, such as a film, stage play, literary property or dance, or specific careers, or to promote appreciation of a particular art form? If the interest promoted is to be private, a regular corporation or partnership or sole proprietorship may be more appropriate than a not-for-profit corporation for several reasons. First, if the economic benefits of an organization seem to be accruing to a closed circle of people, it may be difficult to obtain an exemption from income tax for the organization. For example, if an individual has a corporation in his/her own name and is a director, officer, performer, or employee of the corporation, the aggregation of these several roles in one person may suggest to the Internal Revenue Service that the corporation lacks a donative intent or charitable purpose and that it is organized primarily for private gain. So too, if the activity proposed for an organization is indistinguishable from regular commercial ventures, such as an art gallery that sells work, a management agency selling its services, or a film intended for commercial distribution. To gain exemption, an organization must demonstrate that beyond the personal benefit which may come to its employees, the *public* is also benefiting, in a way that it does not benefit from ordinary tax-paying businesses. This will be explained more carefully later, but if one of the reasons for incorporating not-for-profit is to become tax exempt, and that tax exemption is unlikely, then not-for-profit incorporation may be unwise.

The second reason follows from the assumption that those who intend to promote their own talents through an organization also hope that the economic rewards which accrue as a result of the organization's activities will go to them. This may be difficult for a not-for-profit corporation. Salaries are restricted to what is "reasonable", which may be very generous and comfortable, but possibly not enough to pass all the earnings resulting from an individual's work through the corporation to the individual. Additionally, it may be difficult or impossible to pass the assets of a not-for-profit corporation when it is dissolved onto anything other than another not-for-profit corporation, thereby preventing a sole proprietorship, partnership or regular corporation controlled by an individual from obtaining the rewards at that time. As a condition for recognizing an organization as exempt from income tax, the Internal Revenue Service requires that the corporation have in its articles of incorporation a statement that all the assets of the corporation go to another tax exempt organization when the first is dissolved. Most state laws also require that assets held for a charitable purpose must pass to organizations operated for a simiilar purpose. Of course one always takes one's reputation, knowledge, experience, personal contacts and other such intangibles along wherever one goes, but if you feel that the project you are beginning will go gangbusters, and you want to retain complete economic control of the rewards of that success, a not-for-profit corporation is inappropriate.

Another important question to ask is: Will this enterprise be self-sustaining, or will it need to rely on financial assistance from other sources? And, if financing from other sources is necessary, what are the likely sources available to the organization, given its purpose and composition? Will the corporation be able to obtain gifts and grants, or will it be more likely to attract investors interested in a financial return? If a group is able to be self-sustaining, there may be no need to become tax exempt, and perhaps the economic rewards and the greater freedom permitted to for-profit organizations may make another structure preferable. If the project to be undertaken involves exploiting a single property, such as a motion picture, stage show, or novel, gifts and grants are less likely to be available while private investor interest may be high. A limited partnership might therefore be the appropriate form of organization. Non-commerical ventures likely to attract gifts and grants may be more appropriately conducted by not-for-profit corporations. The point is that each venture must be examined by itself, and that financial considerations are often critical. Only after considering these matters can the decision whether to incorporate not-for-profit be made.

Other Forms of Organization

In order to place the discussion of not-for-profit corporations in a context, this section will outline the basic forms of business organization.

The three primary methods of business organization are the sole proprietorship, the partnership, and the corporation. A *sole proprietor* is the sole owner of his or her business, such as an independent artist or free-lance designer. The proprietor may have employees, but these employees have no further economic interest in the business beyond their right to a salary. If you are not an employee, or if you conduct business apart from your responsibilities as an employee, and you do not have a partner and are not a corporation, then you are a sole proprietor. Sole proprietorships do not legally exist apart from their owners, and the personal assets of the owners may be reached by creditors to satisfy the obligations of the proprietorship.

Partnerships are formed when two or more people agree to conduct a business for profit. Although written partnership agreements are the preferred method of organizing, such instruments are often not necessary; partnerships may be formed by verbal agreements and courses of conduct. Partnerships also do not exist apart from the individuals involved as partners, and each partner may be individually liable for the entire debts and obligations of the partnership. Partners are entitled to whatever percentage of the partnership profits the partners have agreed to; no partner is entitled to a salary from the partnership except by agreement of the partners. *Limited partnerships* are a statutory form of partnership that operate primarily as investment vehicles and are used often in the entertainment industry to finance the production of a motion picture or stage show. Limited partners are able to limit their personal liability for partnership obligations to the amount of their capital contribution to the partnership, but they in return are not allowed to manage in any manner the affairs of the limited partnership. *Associations* may be thought of as large partnerships organized about a constitution or articles of association.

Corporations, which are the favored, contemporary form of conducting business, are of two types: regular and not-for-profit. Both are created by the issuance of a charter by the state in which the corporation is formed. Corporations may be thought of as fictional legal persons which exist apart from the directors, officers and employees who run them. They can own property and assume obligations in their own name, sue and be sued, have perpetuity of life, and incur their own tax obligations. Regular corporations issue shares of stock which, when sold, provide the corporations with capital to conduct their business. The shareholder in turn becomes the owner of the corporation to the extent of his ownership of outstanding shares. Shareholders have the right to vote for the board of directors of the corporation, who in turn elect the officers. The officers manage the day-to-day operations of the corporation and hire additional employees. Dividends are paid to the shareholders from the corporation's earnings. The shareholders, as owners of the corporation (this can be a strained use of the word "owner" in the case of large corporations) are not personally liable for corporate obligations and liabilities except under unusual circumstances. In small corporations formed to conduct the business of one to a dozen people, the shareholders, directors, officers and employees may all be the same group of people.

The most basic differnce between regular corporations and not-for-profit corporations is the fact that not-for-profit corporations either have no shareholders, or, if shareholders are allowed, the corporation is not allowed to pay dividends to these shareholders. While not-for-profit corporations in states which prohibit shareholders may issue membership certificates which confer certain rights and privileges, these members are not entitled to a share of the net earnings of the corporation. Not-for-profit status does not require operation on a cost-recovery basis only; a not-for-profit corporation may make a profit from its activities and pay reasonable compensation for services rendered to it and other reasonable expenses of operating. Since not-for-profit corporations either have no shareholders or are prohibited from paying dividends, however, the net earnings of the corporation must therefore be retained by the corporation to further the purposes for which it was formed.

Steps in the Incorporation Process
Assuming that your group has decided to incorporate not-for-profit, some of the first issues to resolve will be the corporation's name, the identity of the initial board of directors and registered agent, and the purposes of the corporation. Most states require that this information be included in the organization's articles of incorporation, which

operate as a combination legal description/birth certificate for the corporation. The articles give substance to the corporation by empowering it to act in certain manners and pursue certain purposes while prohibiting it from others. The articles provide a limit, however broad, on the scope of the activities of the corporation.

Generally, each state requires that the name of a not-for-profit corporation be in the English language, not identical to or confusingly similar to the name of another corporation operating in the state, and not misdescriptive of the purpose or functions of the corporation. Usually a name may be reserved for up to sixty days before incorporation, allowing an individual or group with a name important to them time to properly prepare organizational papers if that is necessary. While non-English language names are prohibited, acronyms constructed of a foreign language name may be adopted. For example, in Illinois, an arts organization devoted to increasing the public interest in and appreciation of Latin American Artists, called Movimineto Artistico Chicano, was incorporated as MARCH. Initials are also sometimes permissible.

Incorporation also gives an organization some protection for its name to the extent that a state may refuse to incorporate another group with a name confusingly similar. However, the greater protection for an organization's name in connection with its products or services arises through that organization's *use* of its name and proper state and federal trademark registration. While trademarks and how they are obtained will not be discussed here (consult a trademark attorney if name protection is important) it will be noted that although names may be protectable by legal means, they cannot be protected by copyright statutes. Note also that if a corporation does business under a name other than the one under which it was incorporated, it may have to register with either the state or local government that it is doing business under an assumed name.

Most states require that there be at least three members of the initial board of directors of a not-for-profit corporation.

The reason for this is that one person is therefore prevented from having complete legal control of the corporation; any one director may be outvoted by the other two. While we know that in real life one person may have practical control of a whole room of people, this legal requirement remains. The responsibilities and liabilities of directors will be explained below. While three may be the minimum, in most cases only judgment will set the upper limit on the number of directors. Groups that are successful in attracting community support, talent, and funds will have larger boards reflecting the interests and skills they wish to obtain. As will be explained later, obtaining tax exempt status may also be easier with an expanded board. Often it is the scope of one's project and the speed with which one wishes to see it implemented that will determine when, if ever, the initial three board members are increased.

Not-for-profit corporations are required to designate one person as a registered agent and a registered office within the state of incorporation or operation to receive communications from the state and to be served with a summons for suit in the event that other service is unavailable or inappropriate. In most instances, when an attorney prepares your articles of incorporation, and when the registered office need not be the same as the principal office of the corporation, that attorney will designate himself as the agent. This is a recommended practice if the attorney is to continue as counsel for the corporation, for he will be in the best position to evaluate correspondence addressed to the corporation. If the attorney will not continue as counsel, another person must be designated, which may be one of the original board members.

The articles of incorporation will also contain a statement of the corporation's purpose. This section of the articles is the most critical, and if not properly worded, may cause an organization to fail to be recognized as exempt. In most states, in order to successfully incorporate, it is legally sufficient merely to state the corporation's purposes in language which follows the phrasing of the state's not-for-profit corporation statute. Each state specifies the purposes for which a not-for-profit corporation may be formed. These purposes are usually charitable, educational, religious, civic, benevolent, agricultural, fraternal, or something of that kind. A theatre company, for example, could describe its purposes merely as "charitable" or "educational" and successfully incorporate. Problems will arise, however, when such a corporation attempts to gain tax exemption. The reason for this is that the Internal Revenue Service requires greater limitations on a corporation's purposes and activities than the state's not-for-profit corporation laws require. One previously mentioned example is that state law may require that the assets of a not-for-profit corporation at dissolution go only to other not-for-profit corporations. The IRS more narrowly requires that the assets go only to other tax-exempt organizations. Because the IRS is more restrictive, additional paragraphs must be added to a not-for-profit corporation's articles of incorporation to limit the corporation's power to act in accordance with those purposes for which the IRS will grant an exemption. This language usually tracks language found in relevant sections of the Internal Revenue Code. Of course, if tax exemption is not desired, a corporation would be unnecessarily limited by including the corporate purposes required by the IRS.

Assuming that the basic state not-for-profit corporation laws and the IRS requirements, if applicable, have been complied with, other provisions may be added to the articles. For example, an organization may wish to embellish its statement of purpose with language stating the corporation's high aspirations for quality, achievement and public service. This language must be carefully worded, however, to avoid suggesting that the corporation will be conducting a regular business which may be prohibited by the state's not-for-profit law. The standards by which these articles are measured to determine whether purposes are proper may at times seem inexplicable. For example, in Illinois a theatre company was allowed to incorporate with the following among its purposes: "to establish and maintain a theatre company to perform and present theatrical plays, dramas, musical revues and other productions of all kinds, with a particular focus on theatre for children." However, a folk-music society was forced to delete the following· purpose before it could incorporate: "to establish and maintain a publishing company to publish and distribute both new and original and newly rediscovered musical compositions, literary works, and other works of authorship for the education and enlightenment of the general public and for the development, encouragement and exposure of writers whose creative expression may or may not be considered for publication elsewhere." The distinction drawn by the state to determine that establishing a theatre company did not connote doing business but establishing a music publishing company did was lost on this writer, but similar eccentricities may arise in your own state. Also be alert to the consequences of indicating that the corporation will be teaching courses or classes. It is sometimes advisable to state that the corporation will not operate as a trade, vocational or business school, for such activity usually requires special licensing from the state. Degree awarding institutions are also usually regulated by the state and require special approval to operate. Indicating that the corporation will conduct less formal workshops and seminars does not raise any educational licensing issues. Depending on a state's not-for-profit statutes, additional provisions in the articles relating to membership, directors, officers and other by-law type regulations for the corporation may be included.

When the articles of incorporation for each state have been completed, they are usually filed with the office of the Secretary of State, where they are examined for compliance with the state's rules and regulations. The Secretary of State will then issue a charter representing the creation of the legal status of the corporation. This charter must often also be filed with the clerk of the county in which the registered office of the corporation is located.

After the incorporation is completed, the initial board of directors of the corporation will meet to conduct the first business of the newly created not-for-profit corporation. At this meeting several important actions will typically be taken. First, the corporation's by-laws will be adopted. If there are provisions in those by-laws for the selection of additional or new directors, that action will also be taken. It is common at this time for checking accounts to be authorized, seals adopted, debts arising from the process of incorporating to be assumed by the corporation and the treasurer ordered to pay them, authorization given to proceed with applying for recognition of tax-exemption, officers elected, if that is the method stated in the by-laws, leases approved, and membership certificates adopted and issued if the corporation has members. All these actions will be noted in the corporation's minutes, which may be kept in a bound book available at most stationery stores. It will be important to maintain adequate and complete records of board meetings and official corporate acts to demonstrate that the corporate formalities have been observed and that the corporation operated as a separate entity rather than as the alter ego of the individuals involved. This is important for maintaining the limited liability that directors and officers share for the liabilities and obligations of the corporation.

By-Laws

The by-laws of a corporation structure its internal method of operation. They are the rules of order, dictating how the corporation's affairs will be conducted and what rights and responsibilities are to be assumed by the different people involved with the corporation. The following are typical by-law categories with explanations of the considerations one might take into account in choosing one's own by-law provisions.

Directors—What are the requirements for becoming a director? Legally, there may be a few qualifications imposed by a state. In Illinois, for example, directors need not be residents of the state or members of the corporation unless the by-laws or articles so require. The by-laws might require residence in a specific area such as a county or municipality, a certain age range, special interests or skills, or the achievement of a special status or professional accomplishment. These qualifications will depend solely on the intentions of the incorporators. Just as the board of a regular corporation may be structured to reflect the powers and interests of the corporation's principal shareholders, so the board of a not-for-profit corporation may be structured to reflect the various organizations, communities or interests which the corporation wishes to represent. This may be accomplished by stipulating that certain directorships be occupied by individuals representing the various categories the corporation feels are important.

How many directors will there be? How will they be elected? If the corporation has members, will they elect the directors, or will the directors elect themselves, becoming a self-perpetuating board? In Illinois, members have no constitutional right to vote for directors; the members' voting rights are fixed by the articles or the by-laws. What is the term of office for a director? Will there be variable terms, or will the election of portions of the board be staggered so that the board does not completely turn over at each election? If the board has been divided into several categories requiring different types of people in each, the categories could have variable terms, therefore allowing a preferred category to gain greater board power through their longer term of office. How are directors replaced if they leave before their term expires? How may directors be removed? What are the responsibilities of a director? How often do they meet, and how is notice of the meeting provided? How may special meetings be called? Will the directors be paid? Will there be an Executive Committee of the board of directors to conduct some of the business of the board? What are the quorum requirements for board action? Many state's statutes provide answers to these questions in the absence of by-law provisions to the contrary, or set guidelines which the by-laws may follow. In Illinois, for example, a quorum of the directors shall be a majority unless otherwise provided for, provided that in no event may a quorum consist of less than one-third of the directors.

Members—Will the corporation have members? If so, what rights will they have? Will they elect directors or officers, be entitled to vote on amendments to the by-laws or articles, will they have no voting rights at all? Will membership certificates be issued? May these certificates be transferred? (In Illinois, mere possession of a membership certificate will not entitle the holder to membership status when there are further qualifications to be met.) What are the qualifications for membership? Geographical location, age, interest, skill, achievement? How are members accepted or rejected? May members be expelled and, if so, for what reasons? How are members reinstated? Are there different categories of membership? Will there be dues? When do members meet, if ever; where do they meet, and what are the notice requirements of the meeting? How may special meetings be called? What are the quorum and voting requirements for members' meetings? May members vote by proxy, and how?

Generally, it will be preferable for smaller cultural organizations to be non-membership corporations or, if there are members, to specify that they have no voting rights. This permits centralization of decision-making authority in the board of directors and allows the board to structure itself by self-election according to the needs which it recognizes. An example of poor membership planning arose with an unadvised Illinois theatre company which made everyone who appeared in a production a member with voting rights. There were no provisions for membership termination. When it was necessary to submit a proposal to the membership, the theatre found they faced an enormous logistical problem in locating everyone and obtaining a quorum for a membership meeting. They needed to convince the membership of the merit of the proposal in question. The point is that granting members voting rights should be considered carefully, for not only does the organization assume the burden of maintaining membership lists, but those who are the founders of the group and who may have been setting an aesthetic policy unencumbered may find some of their decisions being submitted for group consideration. Just as a cow is a horse designed by committee, so is an arts organization directed by egalitarian notions of consensus likely to produce creative sows.

Even if a group has no members, it is not prevented from soliciting individual supporters who contribute to the organization in return for certain privileges such as seating or admission priority, gifts, receiving a newsletter, etc. In many instances, these persons may be called *members, subscribers, associates* or a similar name without acknowledging their existence formally in the organization's by-laws. If informal membership is important for your organization, consult an attorney to see whether it is legal in your state.

Officers—What are the officers of the corporation, what are their responsibilities, terms of office, how are they elected, how are they removed or replaced, will they be paid, and what qualifications do they need?

In Illinois, by statute, a corporation shall have a president, one or more vice-presidents, a secretary, a treasurer, and other such officers and assistant officers as are deemed necessary. They may be elected in any manner for terms not to exceed three years, and one person may hold any two or more offices except president and secretary. Officers may be removed by the persons authorized to elect or appoint such officers whenever in their judgment the best interests of the corporation will be served thereby.

A president is typically the chief executive officer of the corporation who supervises and conducts the activities of the corporation. Vice-presidents perform duties assigned to them by the president or board of directors. The secretary is generally responsible for maintaining corporate minutes, giving and serving all notices of the corporation, and acting as custodian of the corporate records and seal. The treasurer keeps a record of the receipts and disbursements of the corporation and is responsible for providing financial reports and statements. These officers may be responsible for the day-to-day operation of the corporation, or an executive director—a staff position—may be created to handle and carry out these responsibilities.

Committees—What committees will the corporation have, if any? Will there be any standing committees? What will be their responsibilities? Who will be on the committees and how will they be chosen? What will be the terms of the committees? Who will chair them, how will vacancies be filled, what are the voting and quorum requirements for the committees? In Illinois, it is possible to form a committee of directors with two or more directors to act with the authority of the entire board except in certain major areas, such as amending the by-laws. Other committees may be formed as the board deems necessary.

Special Boards—A corporation may wish to form special boards, such as a board of sponsors or an auxiliary board, which will provide services to the corporation as the board of directors delegates. These are non-decision-making groups, except as necessary in fulfilling the responsibilities delegated to them. Such boards are frequently used in fund-raising efforts. Qualifications for membership on these boards may be determined by the corporation, but it is preferable to have the board of directors select the members of the affiliate board or boards, perhaps upon the recommendation or nomination of the affiliate board.

Amendments—How will the articles of incorporation or by-laws of the organization be amended? By whose vote, members or directors? What voting margins are necessary to amend? In Illinois the articles of incorporation may be amended by an affirmative vote of two-thirds of the members, if they have voting rights, or a majority of the directors. The by-laws may be amended as the by-laws specify, such as by a majority, two-thirds, or three-fourths margin.

Miscellaneous Provisions—What is the corporation's fiscal year? Where are the corporation's offices and where are the books kept? What are the purposes of the corporation? (This provision may repeat the language of the articles or may expand upon it.) What are the procedures for mergers or consolidations? How may the corporation be dissolved? Will the corporation indemnify its directors and officers? These and any other rules which the corporation wishes to adopt to regulate its internal organization, and which are not inconsistent with the articles of incorporation, may become part of the by-laws of the organization. The incorporators should also attempt to envision conflicts which might arise given the special purposes, activities or makeup of the corporation. These conflicts should be capable of resolution by procedures adopted in the by-laws.

It quite often happens that disputes arise within an organization that are not resolved amicably by reference to the by-laws, or there is disagreement on how the by-laws should be construed or whether they have been fairly complied with. A legal action might therefore be brought seeking relief for a complaining party or the proper interpretation which the by-laws should be given. Courts are usually reluctant to interfere with an organization's internal affairs. They will, however, grant relief to members against by-law provisions that are unreasonable or contrary to law or public policy. Members may also seek relief to insure that fair procedures for such things as expulsion and censure established by by-law provisions are complied with, particularly when economic interests are at stake, as well as professional or career enhancement. Generally, however, an organization's by-laws will be the rules by which the organization is run and should be tailored to the needs of the organization. While state statutes may provide a method of procedure in the absence of a by-law provision, an organization's own set of by-laws may be important to change the effect of those statutes to the extent permitted, when such change fits the needs of the organization.

Liabilities of Directors and Officers

The qualities of the board of directors and officers of your corporation will be one of the keys to the success of your organization. A board will be the ultimate decision making group for the corporation, with the authority to make "life and death" kinds of decisions about the corporation such as dissolution, merger, sale of major assets and the like.

As a general rule, directors and officers will not be personally liable for the obligations of the corporation of which they are a part. Because the corporation exists apart from the directors and officers involved with it—with those directors and officers acting on behalf of the corporation—it is the corporation's assets which will be looked to to satisfy the corporation's debts and liabilities. There are instances, however, when directors and officers may face personal liability for actions which they have taken. The following are some examples.

Liability for violation of duty—The duty which directors and officers owe to the corporation is termed a *fiduciary duty,* which means that because they are agents of the corporation, each director and officer must act in the utmost good faith and with due diligence to fulfill the responsibilities of their respective offices. This means that directors and officers cannot secretly profit from their corporate position, cannot acquire an interest in property adverse to the corporation's, cannot use corporate property for personal gain, or in any way act, in their corporate capacity, in a way adverse to the interests of the corporation. Directors and officers will be personally liable for losses which occur to the corporation as a result of a breach of this fiduciary duty due to their negligence, fraud or breach of trust.

The standard by which the acts of directors and officers are measured is called the "business judgment" rule, which means that if a director or officer acts the same as a hypothetically prudent person would under like circumstances, then, even if the act results in loss or harm to the corporation or a third party, the directors or officers will not be personally liable. All business decisions involve risk of failure, but if the decision is made with thought, skill and care, the risk will be borne by the corporation, not the director or officer. This also means that decisions must be informed decisions, and that unquestioned acquiescence to the representations of others, or, in a more extreme example, the abandonment of one's duties in the belief that others will fulfill those responsibilities, will be considered negligent acts. Directors and officers, as a basic duty, must attend meetings and vote on proposals only after becoming fully informed of what they are voting on. They may rely on the reports of experts in seeking to become informed, but again, this reliance must be in good faith.

Liability for ignoring corporate formalities—Because the corporation is a separate legal entity, it must be treated as such by observing what are called corporate formalities. This means that board meetings must be held, by-law provisions followed, corporate funds segregated and not mixed with personal funds, and business conducted with the recognition that the corporation exists apart from the people who serve it. If directors or officers ignore the corporation or treat it as if it were their alter ego, then a court may look to the actual substance of a transaction rather than its form and find that those directors or officers are personally liable for obligations that would otherwise belong to the corporation.

Personal liability on contracts—Because officers and directors are agents for a corporation, they should sign all contracts on behalf of the corporation in their agency capacity. Specifically, instead of simply signing one's name, one would write the name of the corporation first, followed by the word "by", followed by one's signature and then a recitation of one's corporate capacity. For example, "Arts Corporation, by Thomas R. Leavens, Secretary." One's signature alone, in the absence of language indicating that it is really the corporation that is meant to be bound by the contract, may create personal liability for you. In addition, if you misrepresent that you are contracting for yourself and not the corporation, it is obvious that a person who relies on that misrepresenta‹ tion will probably be able to enforce personal liability against you.

Liability for failure to deposit withheld taxes—When your organization begins employing people, it will be required to withhold certain sums of money for income tax payments according to various tax schedules. If such sums are not deposited with the proper tax authorities after they are withheld, the persons responsible for the withholding will be personally liable for such sums not remitted. Although this statutory requirement seems obvious and easy to comply with, many organizations run into severe problems with failure to report. Quite often, a decision is made to defer a tax deposit so that the same money can be used for some other pressing need, such as promotion expenses or rent, with the vow that the tax payment will be made up "soon." Meanwhile, the obligation becomes greater as additional withholding amounts accrue, thereby making the next payment more burdensome. The result is that many groups fall behind and have great difficulty recovering. This author knows of two arts groups, of relatively modest size, which ended up owing back withholding deposits of five figures. Therefore, plan your budget wisely and deposit withholding sums when they are due.

Liability for statutory violations—Most states by statute will prohibit certain acts by corporate directors and officers and impose personal liability or penalties for the harm or loss suffered because of violations of the statute. In Illinois, one may not divert funds owing to or for the account of employees. Loans from the corporation to officers and directors are also prohibited, and those who participate in or vote for such loans are jointly and severally liable for the amount of the loan until it is repaid. There are also criminal penalties that may be imposed upon directors and officers for their failure or refusal to answer interrogations, or written requests for information regarding the corporation requiring written answers, which are propounded to them by the Secretary of State, or for knowingly filing false reports with the Secretary of State. Your own state may have similar or additional statutory provisions, so it would be best to check with an attorney before becoming a director or officer to ascertain those acts which are prohibited in your state.

The act of a director or officer may create liability to a third party, such as a creditor of the corporation, or liability for the expense of defending against such claims, which may be entirely beyond the personal means of that director or officer. In order to attract capable people who might otherwise refuse to serve because of the potentially great liability, some states allow a corporation to indemnify its officers and directors and to purchase indemnification insurance for this purpose. Essentially, indemnification means that if a director or officer actually and necessarily incurs an expense in connection with the corporation, then the corporation will repay them for the expense they have suffered. This indemnification is usually prohibited where liability results from the wilfull misconduct of the director or officer. Check your own state statutes for this provision. Also note that this chapter does not address the rules pertaining to the operation of private foundations, such as the taxes on investment income, excess business holdings, self-dealing transactions, failure to distribute income, the making of investments which jeopardize the charitable purpose of the foundation, and others. These rules are quite complex and beyond the scope of this work. Be advised, however, that if your organization is classified as a private foundation, any officer, director or trustee who has responsibility for a prohibited act under these rules faces heavy personal tax penalties for the violation. Most cultural organizations will not be classified as private foundations, but counsel should be sought to ascertain the status of your organization to avoid this liability if it does apply.

Obtaining and Maintaining Tax-Exemption

The federal government, as a matter of public policy, chooses to encourage certain types of activities through the tax laws. It recognizes that certain organizations operate for a public rather than private gain, and that to burden such organizations with taxes would discourage their formation or that the amount of tax which would be collected from such groups would be small when compared with the greater public benefit which accrues from the operation of the organization. Therefore there has been written into the tax codes an exemption from the payment of income taxes for certain groups formed to further certain favored purposes. These groups are defined in *Section 501(c)* of the IRS Code and number eighteen in all. The category of exemption which most cultural organizations will be concerned with is *Section 501(c)*, which is for organizations "organized and operated exclusively for religious, charitable, scientific, testing for public safety, literary, or educational purposes." While exemptions granted under any of the categories of 501(c) will allow an organization to escape taxation, only donations to organizations recognized as exempt under Section 501(c)(3) will be deductible against ordinary income by the donor. Organizations classified as exempt under Section 501(c)(3) also enjoy special status because of the laws regulating the relationship between foundations and the recipients of their grants. If foundations give grants to any individuals or groups other than a 501(c)(3) organization, then the foundation must undertake fairly rigorous supervisory responsibilities for how that money is used. These responsibilities do not apply to grants to 501(c)(3) groups. Therefore, most foundations, as a matter of policy, elect to give only to 501(c)(3) groups to avoid the extra responsibilities.

What are some of the purposes for which exemption has been granted under Section 501 (c) (3)? The list is long, but some examples include art promotion, apprenticeship training, helping musicians, producing concerts, plays and other works of performing art, dancing schools, career planning, promotion of ceramics, financial management assistance, creative arts grants, discussion groups, and many others. "Organized and operated" means that before exemption will be granted to an organization, the IRS will examine the organization's instruments, meaning its constitution, articles of incorporation, by-laws, or trust agreement, and its activities, or the way in which the organization is actually conducting itself to fulfill its stated purposes. It is possible for an organization to pass the organizational test by having properly worded organizational instruments, but fail the operational test by not operating in the manner the IRS believes organizations should operate which are pursuing exempted purposes.

The IRS does not require an organization to be a corporation before being recognized as exempt. Trusts and associations may also be recognized as exempt. Generally, however, it is advisable for most cultural organizations to incorporate rather than attempt to gain exemption as an association, since the laws dealing with associations are more limited and vague and the structure more informal, making the necessary limitation on activity which the IRS requires more difficult to prove. Moreover, operating as a corporation has the other advantages mentioned earlier in this chapter.

Application for exemption—Exemption is obtained by filing Application Form 1023 with the IRS. This application is more properly termed a notice to the IRS of operation in an exempt manner. If this form is filed within fifteen months of the end of the month in which the organization was formed, the effective date of the exemption, if granted, will be retroactive back to the date of formation. Otherwise the exemption will date from the receipt of the application with the IRS. If an organization exists as an association for several years, then incorporates and files for exemption, the date of formation will be the date of incorporation. If an organization is not a private foundation, which means essentially that less than one-third of its support is derived from investment income and more than one-third of its support is from the public, or, more generally, that the organization is supported by a broad range of public sources, and the gross receipts of the organization are normally not more than $5,000, then the

IRS does not require this notice to be filed. However, as a practical matter, fund raising is impossible without formal recognition of exemption from the IRS, so most organizations file the Form 1023 notice even if they have no receipts whatsoever. Applications typically require two to four months to process and usually require the submission of additional information after the initial application is filed.

The IRS will examine the organization to determine whether it is organized and operated exclusively for the proper purposes. There must be evidence of the donative intent of the organization, and evidence that the activities of the organization will not be engaged in primarily to make a profit, but will be non-commercial in the sense that they are not identical to or do not compete directly with regular commercial enterprises. For example, a typical arts organization, in order to obtain exemption, should be organized to promote appreciation and support of an interest in a certain type of art or to assist promising but unknown artists who may or may not otherwise have the opportunity to exhibit, perform, or publish. If services, information, exhibits or performances are provided, they should be explained to the IRS as not being available elsewhere, generally because of their non-commercial appeal. It is often suggested that an organization adopt an educational component consisting of classes, workshops and the like in skills relating to the arts in which the organization is involved. These technical and educational services should be offered on a cost-recovery or no-charge basis.

These are only general outlines of the types of purposes typically associated with exempt arts organizations. Specifically, a tax-exempt art gallery, for example, may exhibit work, but is not allowed to sell that work or take a commission from the artist for a sale. The gallery may inform visitors how the artist may be contacted directly to make a purchase of an exhibited work, but it may not act as the artist's agent or as a conduit for the sale. A theatre company presenting original drama may find its exemption rescinded if it produces only the works of a few selected directors or officers who also direct, design, produce or perform in the productions. If the benefit of the economic activity of the organization seems to be accruing only to a small group of people, the IRS may consider that the organization lacks a charitable purpose or donative intent. As another example, an organization whose purpose is to produce original television studio drama obtained exemption upon the representation that the distribution of the videotapes so produced would be limited to non-commercial broadcast or cable-cast outlets. Similarly, many arts service organizations obtain exemption only if the services are limited to other not-for-profit or tax-exempt organizations or to those who could not otherwise afford to obtain those services.

The IRS regularly issues revenue rulings which describe certain organizational purposes and activities and then issues a determination whether, given those purposes and activities, tax exemption is appropriate. These revenue rulings serve as guideposts for setting up similar organizations and should be referred to before any application is filed. Although it is not necessary to have an attorney complete and file this application, such assistance is recommended. Obtaining exemption may be critical for your organization, and it would be unfortunate to organize your activities improperly or to misstate your operations to the IRS. New applications may be filed, or appeals taken on rejected applications, but the time lost by such false starts may critically impair the momentum of your emerging group. It is therefore advisable to seek experienced representation prior to your dealings with the IRS.

Maintaining Tax Exemption

When the problems of obtaining tax exemption have been solved, the problems of maintaining this exemption begin. The areas of most concern for organizations are unrelated business income, profit sharing arrangements, and lobbying activities.

Unrelated Business Income—The problem of unrelated business income may be briefly stated as follows: the IRS grants an exemption from the payment of income tax on income earned from activities which further certain favored purposes. However, if the organization conducts other activities constituting a trade or business which are unrelated to the purposes for which the IRS has recognized an exemption, and these activities are regularly carried out, then, under certain circumstances, a tax will be owed on the income earned from the unrelated activities.

For example, assume that a theatre company has been recognized as exempt to present works of performing art and to conduct classes in the theatre arts. Income from these activities would not be taxable. However, if the theatre sold advertising, operated a food store, or conducted some other form of unrelated business, income from these activities would be taxable if the activities were regularly carried out. If the theatre company sold advertising for a program booklet distributed throughout an entire season, for example, the advertising income would be taxable. If the advertising was not regularly sold, however, but was obtained for a booklet distributed at a single event held annually or irregularly, then, while unrelated, the income would not be taxable because the trade or business was not regularly carried out.

Even when a trade or business is unrelated and regularly carried out, income from that activity will be exempt from taxation if 1) it is derived from the sale of donated goods; 2) the people staffing the trade or business are volunteers; or 3) the trade or business is for the benefit of the employees of the organization. For example, if a theatre company regularly operates a second-hand shop selling donated merchandise, the operation is clearly a business and is clearly unrelated. However, the income will not be taxable because the goods are donated. Or, even if the goods were purchased, if the staff of the store were volunteers, again the income would not be taxable. If the same theatre company operated a lunch counter open to the general public that used paid staff and purchased its food, income from that business would be taxable if regularly carried out. However, if the lunch counter was set up for the *employees* of the theatre company, and not for the public, the income would not be taxable.

Income from debt-financed property, such as rent from a building which an organization purchased by taking a mortgage, is also unrelated business income which is taxable.

What does this mean for your own group? The main points to be gained from this are that 1) there are enough variables brought to bear upon the question of unrelated business income to allow creative groups to structure their unrelated activities in a manner which avoids taxation; and 2) it may be necessary to keep separate records of the receipts and disbursements involved with unrelated activity. Also keep in mind that if a tax is imposed, it will be on income, not revenue. Therefore, if you operate on a cost-recovery basis, where expenses equal revenue, there is no income to be taxed Note also that tax will be due only upon unrelated business income in excess of $1,000; the first $1,000 is exempt.

Profit Sharing Arrangements—It quite often happens with tax-exempt performing arts organizations that, upon the successful presentation of a production, they are approached by groups or individuals interested in investing in that production or another production in which they or the investor hold an interest. These offers differ from offers of contributors or gifts to the group, for the expectation is that a profit will be made which will be shared between the investors and the arts group. Such arrangements raise questions about the extent to which tax-exempt groups may engage in profit-sharing activities.

As a basic premise, a tax-exempt organization cannot, other than to an insubstantial amount, engage in activities which are not in furtherance of their exempt purpose. To the extent that a production is a regular commercial enterprise which does not further the corporation's purposes, profit sharing participation might threaten the organization's continued exemption if it becomes a major corporate activity. Certainly, if the resources of a tax-exempt company are continually risked in ventures which result in private profit, the charitable purpose and donative intent of the exempt company might be questioned.

The point is not to advise that profit sharing arrangements should not be undertaken—for they may be very beneficial to a company and are common in the performing arts—or that such plans are sinister, but to suggest caution and counsel in arranging such ventures to avoid undesirable tax consequences. Alternatives to profit sharing may be loan arrangements, purchase of services of the exempt company by the commercial organization, or the licensing of the right to present a production commercially from the exempt company to the commercial company. Competent legal advice should be sought to inform your group of the tax implications of any such venture it enters.

Lobbying—Tax exempt organizations face an absolute prohibition against campaigning on behalf of candidates for public office or contributing to such campaigns, and, until recently, could only lobby if such lobbying activity constituted an "insubstantial" amount of the group's total purpose and activity. While the ban against electoral politics is still the law, the Federal Tax Reform Act of 1976 provided the means by which 501 (c) (3) corporations may now expend up to 20% of their exempt purpose expenditures for lobbying.

In order for an exempt organization to lobby, it must first examine its corporate charter to determine if such lobbying is allowed. Because the prior law allowed only insubstantial lobbying, many corporate charters still include provisions inserted by attorneys limiting the corporation's lobbying activity to satisfy earlier IRS requirements on the matter. If your corporation's charter bans or limits lobbying, an amendment of the charter may be necessary before the corporation may begin the more vigorous lobbying effort now allowed.

Second, the organization must file Form 5768, "ELECTION BY AN ELIGIBLE SECTION 501 (c) (3) ORGANIZATION TO

MAKE EXPENDITURES TO INFLUENCE LEGISLATION", with the IRS. This form notifies the IRS of the group's intentions and will trigger reporting requirements at the end of the year to document this lobbying.

If the lobbying election is made, the organization will be permitted to expend up to 20% of the first $500,000 of its exempt purpose expenditures for the year, plus 15% of the second $500,000, plus 10% of the third $500,000, plus 5% of any additional expenditures—subject to an overall maximum of $1 million for any one year. Lobbying is defined as an expenditure for the purpose of influencing legislation. Within these limitations is a separate limitation for "grass roots" lobbying, which is "any attempt to influence any legislation through an attempt to affect the opinions of the general public or any segment thereof." The limit on grass roots lobbying is 25% of the group's total lobbying expenditure. This means that while 20% of one's expenditures may be used to communicate with legislators or other government officials or employees who may participate in the formation of legislation, only 25% of that amount may be used to communicate with the general public directly. However, to the extent that executive, judicial and administrative bodies such as schools and zoning boards and special authorities do not participate in the formation of legislation, contact with them will not be considered lobbying.

There are other types of activities in which an organization may engage which are not considered to be lobbying. Groups may 1) make available the results of nonpartisan analysis, study or research; 2) provide technical advice or assistance (where such advice would otherwise constitute the influencing of legislation) to a governmental body or to a committee or a subdivision thereof in response to a written request by such body or subdivision; 3) appear before, or communicate to, any legislative body with respect to a possible decision of such body which might affect the existence of the organization, its powers and duties, tax exempt status, or the deduction of contributions to the organization; 4) communicate between it and its bona fide members with respect to legislation or proposed legislation of direct interest to the organization and such members unless these communications constitute grass roots lobbying; and 5) communicate with a governmental official, other than a) a communication with a member or employee of a legislative body (where such communication would otherwise constitute the influencing of legislation) or b) a communication, the principal purpose of which is to influence legislation.

Staff time of an organization will be counted as an expenditure of the organization if the time is paid. Therefore, if there is some question whether your organization will be able to stay within its lobbying limits, and there are volunteer hours to be assigned, it might be advisable to have the volunteers devote their time to the lobbying effort, since their time would not be included within the organization's expenditures. Other expenditures would include telephone, postage, travel and printed material used in the lobbying effort.

Reporting Requirements

The reporting requirements of not-for-profit corporations will of course vary from state to state. There are, however, federal forms which are required of all organizations and some general types of additional reports which may be noted.

If a not-for-profit corporation has not been recognized as tax exempt, it must pay corporate tax at the rates established for regular corporations on its taxable income, subject to the $5,000 exemption mentioned earlier. A 501 (c) (3) exempt organization must file an informational return, an *IRS 990 and Schedule A*, annually on or before the 15th day of the fifth month following the close of the organization's accounting period. If the corporation has unrelated business income exceeding $1,000, then an additional form *IRS-990T* must be filed. If the corporation begins a payroll, then it must begin withholding money for federal tax payments and remitting that money to the IRS. Organizations exempt under Section 501 (c) (3) do not have to make Social Security payments (FICA taxes) unless they *elect* to make payments either by filing *IRS Form SS-15* or by making FICA payments for three consecutive quarters. If the corporation elects Social Security participation, then it will file a quarterly *Return of Withheld Income Tax, IRS Form 941*, due on or before the last day of the month following the last month of the quarter. If it does *not* pay FICA taxes, then it will file a different quarterly report, an *IRS 941E* within the same period. An organization exempt under 501 (c) (3) is also exempt from paying federal unemployement tax.

On the state level, not-for-profit corporations will generally be required to file annual informational returns along with the appropriate withholding payments if there is a state income tax. Liability for state unemployment compensation will also vary from state to state. Generally, not-for-profit corporations must pay into their state's unemployment compensation fund, although many states allow not-for-profit corporations to be self-insurers. This means that instead of paying a regular tax, the corporation only repays to the state those amounts which former employees draw from the compensation fund. Workman's compensation coverage varies from state to state, although generally the activities of most cultural organizations would not be such that state law would require the organization to obtain insurance coverage for its employees. Check with an attorney to see whether your state requires coverage. Of course, with both state unemployement and workman's compensation, a corporation may elect to have coverage even if it is not required by law. In many cases, unions representing performing artists require, as a matter of contract, that an employing corporation provide this coverage for its members before they are allowed to work.

Because one of the important reasons an organization becomes tax exempt is to solicit funds from foundations, government and the general public, such groups should investigate the laws that may exist in their states regarding registering for charitable solicitation and the reporting requirements, if any, which may be imposed. In Illinois, for example, all organizations receiving or attempting to solicit more than $4,000 during any twelve month period ending June 30th of any year must register with the Attorney General. Annual reports are also required, and in some cases, particularly when professional fund raisers are employed, certified audits must be conducted of the organization's records. Moreover, in Illinois, if an organization sends free goods to potential contributors as part of their solicitation, no more than 25% of the total funds raised by such method may go to the manufacturer or supplier of such goods. The Attorney General is also empowered to enjoin fraudulent fund raising schemes and may, in extreme situations, revoke the corporate charter of an organization employing such tactics. Municipalities also typically have provisions regulating street corner and door-to-door solicitation. Fund raising is a sensitive area of public relations and the law of your own state should be carefully complied with to avoid the possible embarrassment or distrust which a finding of non-compliance might cause.

Summary
In sum, forming and operating a not-for-profit corporation requires special knowledge and a commitment to undertaking certain functions with a sense of business order and practice that may or may not have been apparent in the initial excitement of thinking about forming a group. Don't let business handicap your creative activity. If business intrudes or hampers your creative effort, recognize that it nevertheless needs to be taken care of and bring someone into the organization who can deal with it. But don't ignore sound business and legal practices, for the result will generally be the loss of the creative vehicle that you've worked to create.

Thomas R. Leavens